KATSUNO'S REVENGE
and Other
Tales of the Samurai

ASATARO MIYAMORI

DOVER PUBLICATIONS, INC.
Mineola, New York

Bibliographical Note

This Dover edition, first published in 2006, is a slightly abridged edition of *Tales of the Samurai and "Lady Hosokawa," a historical drama; stories illustrating Bushido, the moral principles of the Japanese Knighthood.* Enlarged and Revised Edition. Kelly & Walsh: Yokohama, Japan, 1920. "Lady Hosokawa" and "Press Opinions on the First Edition" have been omitted from the present volume. In addition, eight color plates, originally spaced throughout the text, have been combined in one 8-page insert.

International Standard Book Number: 0-486-44742-1

Manufactured in the United States of America
Dover Publications, Inc., 31 East 2nd Street, Mineola, N.Y. 11501

Preface

The following tales of the samurai, the knights of old Japan, are based largely on real facts. They have been adapted from among traditional stories related by *kōdanshi*, story-tellers, who nightly delight large audiences with romances and historical stories, especially the noble deeds of the samurai. There are also numerous Japanese books and magazines devoted to stories of this description, which are read with keen interest by all classes of our countrymen, in particular by young people.

It is true the samurai class has gone forever along with feudalism; but fortunately or unfortunately the Japanese at large are samurai in a sense. During the last half century European civilization has revolutionized Japanese society, both for better and for worse. In institutions political and social, in manners and customs, in arts and literature, the Japanese have lost many of their characteristics; yet it may safely be said that the sentiments, motives and moral principles of the samurai in some measure remain in the bedrock of their character, in their subconsciousness, so to speak. The Japanese of to-day are intellectually almost cosmopolitans, but emotionally they are still samurai to no small degree.

Honest Kyūsuké, the hero of the story of the same title, was not a samurai, but his principles were those of a samurai. Let that justify the inclusion of the story in this volume.

The author's hearty thanks are due to Mr. Joen Momokawa, a celebrated *kōdanshi*, who kindly helped him in the choice of these tales, and also to the editor of the *Kōdan Kurabu* for permission to translate *Katsuno's Revenge*, one of his stories.

Tokio, December, 1920.   A. Miyamori.

Contents

v

UNGO-ZENJI

Ungo-Zenji

IT was snowing fast.

Already as far as eye could see the world was covered with a vast silvery sheet. Hill and dale, tree and field, all alike clothed in virgin white.

Caring nothing for the bitter cold, but loving the beautiful, Daté Masamuné determined to go out to enjoy the scene. Accordingly, accompanied by a few attendants, he wended his way to a pavilion set on a low hill in the castle grounds whence an extensive view, embracing the whole of his little fief of Osaki, could be obtained.

In later life Masamuné distinguished himself by signal service rendered to the state, eventually becoming one of the greatest daimios in Japan, under Iyeyasu, the first Shogun, but at this time Osaki was his sole estate, and his income did not exceed 100,000 *koku* of rice a year.

"What an enchanting picture! What can compare with a snow landscape?" he exclaimed, as he stood enraptured, gazing with delight from the balcony of the pavilion at the pure loveliness of the scene before him. "It is said that snow foretells a fruitful year. When the harvest is abundant great is the rejoicing of the people, and peace and prosperity reign over the land!"

While his lordship thus soliloquized, Heishiro, the sandal-bearer—Makabé Heishiro as he was called from his birthplace, Makabé in Hitachi, a surname being a luxury unknown to the third estate—waited without. Having adjusted his master's foot-gear there was nothing more to do till he should come out again.

But presently Heishiro observed that the snowflakes fell and lay somewhat thick on his valuable charge. He hastened to brush them off with his sleeve, but more flakes fell, and again the *geta* (clogs) were covered with icy particles.

"This will never do," he said to himself. "His lordship disdains to wear *tabi* (socks) even in the coldest weather, deeming it a mark of effeminacy; should he place his bare feet on these damp *geta* he will assuredly catch cold. I must keep them warm and dry for him."

So the good fellow in the kindness of his simple heart took up the heavy wooden clogs, and putting them in the bosom of his garment next his skin, continued his patient waiting.

"His lordship comes!"

Heishiro had just time to put the *geta* straight on the large stone step at the entrance before the double doors slid open right and left and Masamuné appeared, young, imperious.

He slipped his feet on to the *geta*. How was this? They felt warm to his touch! How could that be in such freezing weather? There could be but one explanation. That lazy lout of a sandal-bearer had been using them as a seat—sitting on the honourable footgear of his august master! The insufferable insolence of the fellow!

In a passion at the supposed insult he caught the offender by the nape of his neck, and shook him violently, exclaiming between his set teeth, "You scoundrel! How dared you defile my *geta* by sitting on them! You have grossly insulted me behind my back! Villain, take that. . . ."

Catching up one of the clogs which he had kicked off, he struck the poor servitor a heavy blow between the eyes, which caused him to reel stunned and bleeding to the ground. Then hurling the companion *geta* at his prostrate victim, he strode proudly back to the castle, barefooted, for he was in too great a rage to wait until another pair of *geta* could be brought.

No one stayed to look after Heishiro. None cared what became of him. For some time he lay as he had fallen, but presently the cold brought him back to consciousness, and he rose slowly and with difficulty to his feet.

He picked up the *geta* with which he had been struck, and

with tears mingling with the blood on his face gazed at it mournfully for a few moments. Then, as the thought of his master's injustice came over him, he gnashed his teeth in impotent rage.

"Haughty brute, that you are, Masamuné," he muttered, "you shall pay for this! The bond between us as lord and vassal has snapped for ever. I have been one of the most devoted of your humble servants, but now I will never rest till I have had my revenge on you for this cruel treatment!"

Then Heishiro again put the *geta* into his bosom, though with how different an intention from before, and descending the hill on the side furthest from the castle, limped painfully away.

From that time forth the man had but one idea—to wreak condign vengeance on the arrogant noble who had so abused his kindness.

But Masamuné was a daimio, through a poor one, while Heishiro was only a serf. Assassination was impossible, Masamuné being always well guarded even while he slept, besides possessing considerable bodily strength himself. He must have recourse to other and subtler means. He thought long and deeply. There were only two persons of higher rank than the daimio who could affect his position at will—the Emperor and the Shogun. But how could a man of Heishiro's standing gain the ear of either of these two illustrious personages so as to slander Masamuné and influence them against him? The very idea was absurd! True, it was a warlike age and promotion speedily followed the achievement of a deed of valor; with a spear in his hand and a good horse under him one might rise to almost any height. But Heishiro was no soldier and his physical strength was small. With a sigh he admitted to himself that the accomplishment of his purpose did not lie that way.

And then a happy thought struck him. He remembered that any one, high or low, great or small, could become a priest and that the prospects held out in that profession were boundless. There was no distinction to which a man of the lowliest parentage and the weakest body might not aspire. A learned priest with a reputation for sanctity might get access to Court—gain the notice of the Emperor himself!

That was it!

Heishiro resolved to turn priest, and with this in view made all haste to Kyoto, where he entered the Temple of Ungoji in Higashiyama as an acolyte.

But the career of an acolyte is none of the easiest. Before he can be received into the priesthood he must go through all forms of asceticism, self-denial, and penance. Furthermore, he has to serve his superiors as a drudge, doing the most menial tasks at their command. Heishiro had a very hard time of it. A man of ordinary perseverance might have succumbed and given up. Not so Heishiro. Not for a moment did he dream of abandoning his self-imposed task. He was determined as long as there was life in him to endure every hardship and humiliation, so that eventually he might attain his end. Still he was but human, and there were times when his weary body almost gave way and his spirit flagged. His racked nerves seemed as if they could bear no more. At such times he would look in a mirror at the reflection of the deep scar on his brow, and draw from its place of concealment the odd garden *geta,* saying to himself, "Courage! Remember Masamuné! Your work is not done yet."

Then strength and calmness would return and he once more felt equal to labour and endure.

Little by little Heishiro rose in the favour of his superiors, and his learning showed marked progress. At length, he thought he might get on faster if he went to another monastery, and the Temple of Enryakuji on Mt. Hiei being the largest and most renowned of all places of sacred teaching in Japan, he applied there for admission and was readily admitted.

Twenty years later, Jōben, for that was the name Heishiro took on entering the priesthood, was known far and near for his erudition and strict application to all observances of a life of the most austere piety. But he was not satisfied. He was still very far from being in a position to attract the notice of the Emperor. Yet higher must he climb. To be world-famous was his aim.

So he made up his mind to go over to China, justly regarded as the fountain-head of all knowledge and wisdom. All she could impart of the Buddhistic faith he would acquire. As soon as an opportunity offered Jōben sailed from his native shores and found himself among a strange people. Here he remained ten years. During that time he visited many famous temples and gathered wisdom from many sources. At last the fame of the traveller reached the ear of the Chinese Emperor, who was pleased to grant him an audience, and graciously bestowed on him a new sacerdotal name, that of Issan-Kasho-Daizenji. Thus it came about that Jōben left his country acknowledged, indeed to be a wise and holy man, but he came back to be regarded as the foremost divine in Japan.

After his return Issan-Kasho-Daizenji stayed at Ungo-ji, the temple in Kyoto where he had entered on his noviciate. He had heard nothing of Masamuné for some years and was anxious to learn what had become of him. He was unpleasantly surprised to hear that the object of his hatred had also risen in the world, and that now as lord of the Castle of Sendai he was considered one of the most important men of the day. Not only did he hold a high office at Court, but as the head of the North-Eastern daimios, even the Shogun had to treat him with respect. All this was annoying if nothing worse. The Zenji saw that he would have to bide his time and act warily. A false move now might render futile all his long years of travail.

But after all he did not have to wait very long.

The Emperor was taken ill and his malady was of so serious a nature that the skill of the wisest physicians proved of no avail. The highest officials of the Imperial Household met in solemn conclave to discuss the matter as it was decided that earthly means being vain the only hope lay in an appeal to Heaven.

Who was the priest of character so stainless, of wisdom so profound that he might be entrusted with this high mission?

One name rose to all lips—"Issan-Kasho-Daizenji!"

With all speed, therefore, the holy man was summoned to the Palace and ordered to pray his hardest to the Heavenly Powers for the restoration to health of the Imperial patient.

For seven days and seven nights the Zenji isolated himself from all mankind in the Hall of the Blue Dragon. For seven days and seven nights he fasted, and prayed that the precious life might be spared. And his prayers were heard. At the end of that time the Emperor took a turn for the better, and so rapid was his recovery that in a very short time all cause of anxiety about him was over.

His Majesty's gratitude knew no bounds. The Zenji was honoured with many marks of the Imperial regard, and as a consequence, all the ministers and courtiers vied with each other in obsequiousness to the favourite of the Emperor. He was appointed Head of the Ungoji Temple, and received yet another name, Ungo-Daizenji.

"The attainment of my desire is now within reach!" thought the priest exultantly. "It only remains to find a plausible pretext for accusing Masamuné of high treason."

But more than thirty years had elapsed since Makabé Heishiro, the lowly sandal-bearer, had vowed vengeance on the daimio Daté Masamuné, and not without effect had been his delving into holy scriptures, his long vigils, his life of asceticism and meditation. Heishiro had become Ungo-Daizenji, a great priest. His character had undergone a radical change, though he had not suspected it. His mind had been purified and was now incapable of harbouring so mean and paltry a feeling as a desire for revenge. Now that the power was in his grasp he no longer cared to exercise it.

"To hate, or to try to injure a fellow-creature is below one who has entered the priesthood," he said to himself. "The winds of passion disturb only those who move about the maze of the secular world. When a man's spiritual eyes are opened, neither east nor west, neither north nor south exists—such things are but illusions. I have nursed a grudge against Lord Daté for over thirty years, and with the sole object of revenge before my eyes have raised myself to my present position. But if Lord Daté had not ill-treated me on a certain occasion, what would my life have been? I should, probably, have remained Heishiro, the sandal-bearer, all my days. But my lord had the unkindness to strike me with a garden *geta* without troubling himself to find out whether I deserved such chastisement. I was roused to anger and vowed to be revenged. Because of my resolve to punish him I turned priest, studied hard, endured privations, and so, at length, have become one of the most influential priests in the Empire, before whom even princes and nobles bow with reverence. If I look at the matter in its true light it is to Lord Daté that I owe everything. In olden times Sakya Muni, turning his back upon earthly glory, climbed Mt. Dantoku and there served his noviciate with St. Arara. Prince though he was, he performed all menial offices for his master, who if ever the disciple seemed negligent, would beat him with a cane. 'How mortifying it is,' thought the Royal neophyte, 'that I, born to a throne, should be treated thus by one so far beneath me in rank.' But Sakya Muni was a man of indomitable spirit. The more humiliations he had to suffer the more earnestly did he apply himself to his religious studies, so that, at the early age of thirty he had learnt all his teacher could impart, and himself began to teach, introducing to the world one of the greatest religions it has ever known. It may truthfully be said that Sakya's success was largely, if not wholly, due to that stern and relentless master who allowed no shirking of his work. Far be it from me to institute any comparison between my humble self and the holy Founder of Buddhism, but, nevertheless, I cannot deny the fact that the pavilion in the grounds of Osaki Castle was my Mt. Dantoku, and this old garden *geta* my St. Arara's cane. Therefore, it should be gratitude, not revenge, that I have in my heart for Masamuné, for it was his unconsidered act that laid the foundation of my prosperity."

Thus the good priest relinquished his long cherished idea of vengeance, and a better feeling took its place. He now looked upon the blood-stained *geta* with reverence, offering flowers and burning incense before it, while day and night he prayed fervently for the long life and happiness of his old master, Lord Daté Masamuné.

And Masamuné himself?

As stated above he attained great honours and became a leading man in the councils of his country. But at the age of sixty-three he tired of public life and retired to pass the evening of his days at his Castle of Sendai. Here, to employ his leisure, he set about the restoration of the well-known temple of Zuiganji, at Matsushima, in the vicinity of the castle, which during a long period of civil strife had fallen into decay, being in fact a complete ruin. Masamuné took it upon himself to restore the building to its former rich splendor, and then when all was done looked about for a priest of deep learning and acknowledged virtue who should be worthy to be placed in charge of it.

At a gathering of his chief retainers he addressed them as follows:—

"As you know I have rebuilt and decorated the Zuiganji Temple in this vicinity, but it still remains without a Superior. I desire to entrust it to a holy and learned man who will carry on its ancient traditions as a seat of piety. Tell me, who is the greatest priest of the day?"

"Ungo-Zenji, High Priest of the Ungoji Temple in Kyoto is undoubtedly the greatest priest of the day," came the unanimous reply.

So Masamuné decided to offer the vacant post to the holy Ungo-Daizenji, but as the priest in question was a favourite at Court, and enjoyed the confidence of the Emperor, it was necessary that His Majesty should first be approached before anything was said to the Zenji. Masamuné tendered his petition in due form and as a personal favour to himself. The Emperor, who retained a warm affection for the retired statesman, readily assented, and thus it came about that Ungo-Zenji was appointed Head of the Zuiganji Temple in the beautiful district of Matsushima.

On the seventh day after his installation, Masamuné paid a formal call at the Zuiganji to welcome the new arrival. He was ushered into the private guest-room of the Zenji which was at the moment unoccupied. On turning to the alcove his attention was at once arrested by the sight of an old garden *geta* placed on a valuable stand of elaborate and costly workmanship.

"What celebrated personage has used that *geta*?" said the astonished Masamuné to himself. "But surely it is a breach of etiquette to decorate a room with such a lowly article when about to receive a daimio of my standing! However, the priest has doubtless some purpose in allowing so strange an infringement of good manners."

At that moment the sliding door opened noiselessly, and a venerable man in full canonicals and bearing a holy brush of long white hair in his hand, came in. His immobile face was that of an ascetic but marred by a disfiguring scar on his forehead between the eyes.

Ungo-Zenji, for he it was, seated himself opposite his guest and putting both hands, palm downwards, on the mats bowed several times in respectful greeting, Masamuné returning the courtesy with due ceremony.

When the salutations were over, Masamuné could no longer restrain his curiosity.

"Your Reverence," he began, "in compliance with my earnest request you have condescended to come down to this insignificant place to take charge of our temple. I am profoundly impressed by your goodness and know not how to thank you. I am a plain man and unskilled in words. But, your Reverence, there are two things which puzzle me, and though at this our first interview you may deem it a want of good breeding to be so inquisitive, may I ask you to explain the place of honour given to a garden *geta,* and the scar on your brow that accords so ill with your reputation for saintliness?"

At these words, poured out with the impetuosity he remembered in Masamuné as a young man, the priest smiled a little. Then he withdrew to the lower end of the apartment and with tears glistening in his sunken eyes, said:—

"How rejoiced I am to see your face again. To gaze upon your unchanged features reminds me of the days of my long past youth."

"What, your words are strange! How can I remind you of your youth, when, to my knowledge, we never met till this day?"

"My lord, have patience, and I will explain all," replied the Zenji. "In those days, I was but a servant—a sandal-bearer known as Makabé Heishiro—it is not likely so humble an individual would retain a place in your memory. It was when you were residing at the Castle of Osaki. . . ."

He paused, but Masamuné, too amazed to utter a word, only looked intently at his former servant as if trying to recall having ever seen him before.

So Ungo-Zenji went on with his story, and in detail told all that had befallen him since that snowy day more than thirty

years before. He did not spare himself, but told how through all
those years he had been actuated by a feeling of revenge and
revenge only, and how the thought of some day seeing his
enemy in the dust had been the spur to goad him on to conquer
all difficulties, to surmount every obstacle.

"At length," concluded the priest, "I came under the notice
of the Emperor who so magnified a trifling service that he
loaded me with rewards and marks of favour. 'Now is my time!'
I thought. But to my own astonishment I found that so vile a
passion no longer existed in my nature—the desire for revenge
had fled. I began to view the affair in a different light, and to
look upon you as my benefactor. But for you I should still be a
sandal-bearer—but for you the stores of knowledge at my command would never have come within my reach—but for you the
intercourse I have had with the illustrious and sage men of two
countries would have been an impossibility. Therefore, my
hatred is turned to gratitude, my wish for vengeance to a heart-
felt desire for your long life and prosperity. I pray daily that
some day I may be enabled in some small measure to requite
the inestimable benefits I owe to you. Your lordship now under-
stands why I so treasure an old *geta,* and how it is I bear this ugly
scar on my brow."

Masamuné listened to the narrative with growing wonder
and the deepest attention. At its conclusion he rose and taking
the Zenji by both hands gently, but forcibly drew him to the
upper end of the apartment. When both were again seated he
spoke.

"Your Reverence," he said in a voice full of emotion. "What
you have just told me quite puts me out of countenance. I can
just recall the incident of which you speak and I remember how
angry I felt at what in my arrogance I deemed a gross insult. I
do not wonder at your desire for revenge, but, that you should
renounce the triumph that was yours for the asking—that,
indeed, amazes me! Such magnanimity is almost incredible! You
prove to me that religion is not the empty abstraction some call
it, and I humbly beg your pardon for my past offence, and
request you to enrol me as one of your disciples."

In this way, Masamuné who was of a frank and noble disposition repented of the fault committed in his youth, and the sandal-bearer achieved a greater victory than he could have boasted of had he caused his enemy to die a shameful death.

A hearty friendship sprang up between the two generous minded men, and till death parted them many years later they saw much of each other and their affection grew. The priest was always a welcome guest at the Castle, while with earnest piety, Masamuné prosecuted his studies in sacred lore under the guidance of Ungo-Zenji.

THE LOYALTY OF A
BOY SAMURAI

The Loyalty of a Boy Samurai

MATSUDAIRA Nobutsuna was one of the ministers of the Shogun Iyemitsu, next to Iyeyasu, the ablest of all the Tokugawa Shoguns. A man of great sagacity, he contributed not a little to Iyemitsu's wise administration.

When Iyemitsu was a young boy named Takechiyo, Nobutsuna who was called at that time Chōshirō served him as one of his attendants and playmates.

One morning when the young nobleman was passing along a corridor accompanied by Chōshirō and two other boys, on the way to the private apartments of his father, the Shogun Hidetada, his attention was caught by some fledgling sparrows that were hopping about and chirping gaily on the tiles of the roof. Takechiyo, then but ten years of age, was seized with a fancy to have them; and turning to Chōshirō, three years older than himself, he commanded:—

"Catch those little sparrows for me, Chōshirō."

"With pleasure, your lordship; but should I be found catching sparrows I should be reprimanded by his Highness and the officials. Fortunately I shall be on duty to-night; so to-night I will climb out on to the roof when there is no one to see me, and give you the little birds in the morning. Will you please to wait till then, my master?"

"I suppose I must." And the small company passed on.

That night when all was quiet, Chōshirō managed somehow or other to get out on to the roof, and crawling carefully on all

15

fours to the spot where the parent birds had built their nest, reached out one hand and seized one of the little sparrows. Poor little things! Surprised in their sleep they were not able to escape. Transferring his captive to the left hand Chōshirō again stretched out his right and caught another. Whether the attainment of his purpose caused him to relax his care or for some other reason, certain it is that at this moment his foot slipped and with a heavy thud he fell down into the courtyard below. As he fell he involuntarily clutched the birds more firmly so that they were instantly squeezed to death. With the dead birds in his hands, he fainted. But the roof was comparatively low, and he also had the good fortune to fall on to some bushes so that he was not killed as might have been the case.

The sound of the fall awoke the Shogun. He started up and followed by his consort and some attendants went out on to the verandah and opening a sliding shutter looked down. By the light of a lantern held by one of the servants he perceived the boy lying on the ground just beneath. Chōshirō had now recovered consciousness and was trying to rise though the pain he felt all over his body rendered the operation one of considerable difficulty. His consternation was great when the light of the lantern revealed his person to those on the verandah.

"Chōshirō, is that you?" called his lord, recognizing the boy at once. "It is strange that you should be on my roof at this time of night! Come up instantly and explain your conduct. This must be inquired into."

The boy, still holding the dead sparrows, obeyed. Prostrating himself before the Shogun he waited for him to speak.

"What have you in your hands, Chōshirō?"

"Sparrows, my lord."

"Sparrows? Do you then climb roofs at midnight to catch sparrows? A strange fancy!"

"Yes, my lord. I will tell you the truth. When Takechiyo Sama and I were passing along the corridor this morning his attention was attracted by some little sparrows on the roof and we stopped to watch them. Takechiyo Sama said 'What dear little things they are!' and the desire then arose in my mind to get them for him that he might play with them. So to-night when everyone was asleep I climbed out on to the roof of your apartments in disregard to the respect I should have shown to your august person, and caught two of the young sparrows. But how quickly the punishment of Heaven followed my crime! I fell down as you see and my wickedness was discovered. I am ready for any chastisement your lordship sees fit to inflict."

"My lord," here broke in Lady Eyo, the Shogun's consort. "Excuse my interference, but I think Takechiyo must have ordered Chōshirō to catch these sparrows. There is no doubt about it."

It should be explained that Lady Eyo had two sons—Takechiyo and Kunimatsu. Takechiyo, the elder, was sharp-witted and active though rather rough in his manners; his brother, on the contrary, was quiet and effeminate. For this and probably some other unknown reason the younger son was his mother's favourite, and it was her desire that he should be appointed heir to the Shogunate in place of his elder brother. She therefore lost no opportunity to disparage Takechiyo in the estimation of his father, hoping thereby to attain her object in due time.

"What a thoughtless boy Takechiyo is!" agreed the Shogun. "This was undoubtedly done at his instigation. How cruel to command Chōshirō to endanger his life by catching birds on a roof at night! Though he is but a child there is no excuse for him. The proverb says 'A snake bites even when it is only an inch long.' One who is so inconsiderate to his attendants when young cannot be expected to govern wisely and well when more power is invested in his hands. Now, Chōshirō," turning to the boy who still knelt at his feet, "Takechiyo ordered you to get the sparrows; is it not so?"

Chōshirō had heard with surprise the unkind words of the Shogun and his lady about his adored master. What did they mean by the words "A snake bites even when it is only an inch long?" If their feelings towards the boy were already so antagonistic what would they think and do should the real facts of the case be disclosed? Chōshirō firmly resolved to take all the blame even at the risk of his life.

"Oh, no, my lord," said he earnestly. "Takechiyo Sama never gave me such a command, never! I caught these sparrows quite of my own accord. I meant one for Takechiyo Sama, and one for myself."

"Nonsense! Whatever you say I know Takechiyo is at the bottom of it. You are a bold fellow to dare to tell me an untruth! . . . Let me see, what shall I do to you? . . . Here, bring me one of those bags."

The Shogun pointed to some large, strong leather bags, resembling a money-pouch in shape, in which in the event of a fire or of an earthquake his valuables would be incased before putting them into the *dozō* or fire-proof godown.

When the bag was brought the Shogun said:—

"Now, Chōshirō, if you don't confess the truth, I will have you put into this bag and never allow you to go home again, nor give you any food. Do you still persist in your falsehood?"

"It is no falsehood, my lord. It is the truth that I caught the sparrows of my own wish. No one but myself is responsible for my misdeed. My fall from the roof was the punishment of Heaven. It is right that you should chastise me also. I beg you to do so."

With these words, Chōshirō, betraying no signs of fear, put himself into the bag.

"What a stubborn boy!" exclaimed the Shogun in anger.

Then with the help of his consort he tightly fastened up the bag with the boy in it, and had it hung from a peg on the wall of the corridor. Leaving the poor child in this state all retired once more to their broken rest.

Late the next morning, having had breakfast and finished her toilet, Lady Eyo, attended by two maids of honour, came out to the corridor where the bag still hung and ordered it to be taken down. On opening it the boy was found still holding the dead sparrows.

"Good morning, your ladyship," said Chōshirō, rubbing his eyes with his closed fists.

"You were ordered by Takechiyo to take the sparrows, is it

not so?" said Lady Eyo kindly, hoping to make the boy confess the truth.

"No, my lady. It was my own idea. Takechiyo Sama had nothing whatever to do with the matter."

"Come, boy, if you are so obstinate you will have to remain a prisoner always, and never have anything to eat. But if you confess what I am convinced is the truth, you shall be released and have food at once. Now tell the truth."

"My lady, as you command me to do so I will tell the truth; but I am so hungry that I find it difficult to speak at all. May I ask for some food first? If you will allow me to have even some *musubi*,* I will say all you wish."

"Good boy, you shall have some *musubi* at once."

The lady gave the order and soon the boy was eagerly devouring the rice-cakes. Three or four large ones made a good meal.

"Thank you, my lady; I am now able to speak."

"Then confess the truth, good boy, confess quickly; I am tired of waiting."

"Forgive me, my lady; I caught the sparrows of my own accord. I received no order direct or indirect from Takechiyo Sama. That is the truth."

The lady for once forgot herself and flew into a passion. Stamping her foot on the floor, she rushed into the Shogun's room and gave him an exaggerated account of what had happened. He was very angry.

"The young rascal," cried he, rising, and taking his Yoshimitsu sword in his hand, "I will kill him myself. Tango Hasegawa, bring Chōshirō here."

Tango found the culprit sitting in the bag his hands onhis lap.

"Chōshirō," he said, "his lordship is terribly angry with you— your stubbornness and insolence are past endurance. He intends to kill you with his own hands. Prepare yourself for instant death!"

"I am quite prepared, sir."

---

*Boiled rice pressed into balls sometimes taken for a simple lunch.

"Your father is my old friend," went on the man pitifully. "If you have any farewell message for him I will undertake to deliver it."

"Thank you, sir; but I have no words to send to my father. It is the duty of a samurai to sacrifice his life for the sake of loyalty. After my death my motive for refusing to confess what my lord the Shogun desires will become clear. Tell my father only that I met my doom fearlessly by my lord's own sword. My one sorrow is that my mother is now ill and this news may lead to her death also. That is my only regret."

"What a truly heroic resolve!" cried Tango, unable to restrain his tears. "Your father may well be proud of you, boy, when I tell him how you met death."

Taking Chōshirō by the hand Tango conducted him into the presence of the Shogun and his lady. The stern noble stood up on their entrance and laying his hand on the hilt of his sword motioned to them to approach nearer. The brave boy kneeling down pushed the stray locks from his neck, and with clasped hands and closed eyes calmly awaited decapitation. The Shogun's manly compassion was not proof against this pathetic sight. Throwing his sword away,

"Chōshirō, you are forgiven!" he cried. "I recognize your supreme fidelity to your young master—faithful unto death! Tango, I foretell that when Takechiyo succeeds me as Shogun, no one will be able to assist him in the task of ruling his people so well as this courageous young samurai. Chōshirō, you are pardoned!"

KATSUNO'S REVENGE

Katsuno's Revenge

A MAN and a woman were whispering to each other by a shaded lamp in a quiet detached room which was partly hedged by *unohana* whose snow-white flowers gleamed in the moonlight. Only the frogs croaking in the neighbouring paddy-field broke the stillness of the night.

The man was Sakuma Shichiroyemon, a councillor of Oda Nobuyuki, the lord of the castle of Iwakura, in the province of Owari. About fifty-two years old, he was a fierce-looking man with powerful muscles and bristling gray whiskers. Haughty, quick-tempered and very jealous he tyrannized over his subordinates and was accordingly an object of hatred throughout the clan. The person with whom he was now talking was a woman close upon his own age—the supervisor of Lord Oda's maids-of-honour, by name O-Tora-no-Kata. Being a cross, cunning, and avaricious hag, she was regarded by the maids with terror and detestation. "Birds of a feather flock together." She had wormed her way into the good graces of Shichiroyemon in order to make her position secure; whilst the latter, on his part, had set her to spy on the actions of his lord, as well as of his colleagues and inferiors.

"What's that, Madame Tora?" asked Shichiroyemon, his face reddening with anger. "Do you mean to tell me that our lord is going to set that green boy of a Hachiya over me as Prime Councillor?"

"I repeat what I hear;—all the maids say so. . . ."

"Pshaw! How I do hate that Hachiya—that peasant's son

23

born in obscurity. Who knows where he comes from? A pale, smooth-faced womanish sprig! How glibly he flatters our lord! He has never been in battle; what use is such a bookworm in these warlike days? And yet this inexperienced stripling is going to be appointed Prime Councillor! Humph, what infatuation! Ha, ha, ha!"

"It will not boil yet. The fire is not strong enough."

"Eh! The fire?"

"Ha, ha!" said O-Tora with a disagreeable smile. "Here I have good fuel to make you burn!"

"Don't try to annoy me like that," said he impatiently. "Tell me quickly."

"It is the secret of secrets. I can't readily . . . w-e-l-l . . . sell it." She spoke slowly, with an emphasis on the word "sell."

"How grasping you are! Well, then, I will buy your secret with this." So saying, Shichiroyemon took a packet of money out of his bosom and threw it down on the mat. The crone picked it up in silence, a cunning smile playing about her lips.

"Mr. Sakuma, you must not be off your guard."

"What do you mean?"

"Well, K . . . ; you must give her up."

"What! Give up Katsuno?" he exclaimed, startled. "Why? Tell me quick!"

"Don't be surprised, sir. It is our lord's pleasure to give her to Hachiya in marriage."

Katsuno was a maid-of-honour of Oda Nobuyuki with whom she was a great favourite. A young damsel of nineteen springs, she was the incarnation of beauty, grace and sweetness of disposition, combined with refinement and dignity. In spite of his years Shichiroyemon was madly in love with the fair maiden; but though he had courted her in every way through O-Tora, she had shown no inclination to respond to his advances.

"Has Hachiya formed a liaison with Katsuno?" asked Shichiroyemon anxiously.

"Not that; you know they are both such honest blockheads; they are too stupid for that. Even if they had the inclination, it would be impossible for them to elude my vigilant eye—not even a devil could do it!"

"Is it then our lord's order?"

"That is it. To-day our lady said to me, 'It is not good for Hachiya to be alone any longer; Katsuno is a beautiful and excellent-minded maid, I will give her in marriage to Hachiya before long in reward for her faithful service!' Yes, surely, our lady told me so."

"Is that indeed so?" said Shichiroyemon, his brow darkening, and his eyes glaring with the intensity of his jealousy. "That green peasant's son of a Hachiya! It would be infamous to put him over a man of my ability and experience, it would be an additional wrong to give Katsuno to him in marriage. What an insult! What mortification to one of my years! I cannot stand it! I shall never rest till I have taken some steps against this Hachiya—my mortal enemy! I will have my revenge! He does not provoke me with impunity!" He spoke so fiercely and the look on his face was so diabolical that the old woman was frightened.

"Your anger is quite natural, sir; but you know 'Anger leads to loss.' You must think more calmly about this matter."

"Have you anything to propose?"

"Well, . . . of course, in the first place Hachiya must be assassinated, and then we must manage to get Katsuno out of the hands of our lord on some pretext or other;—I will undertake *that*."

"And I will settle the other business! But, be careful, Madame Tora!"

Here a puff of cool wind swept through the room and blowing out the light of the lamp put an end to their conference for that time.

II.

It was a fine afternoon in autumn; in the gardens of the castle of Iwakura, the glowing maple leaves and vari-coloured chrysanthemums were in the height of their beauty.

To-day being the anniversary of the death of Nobuyuki's father, all the inmates of the castle had been busy since the early morning with religious services, and a visit to the deceased's grave; to-night a banquet was to be given to all the samurai.

It was now about four o'clock, and several maids-of-honour

who had retired to a private chamber to enjoy an interval of rest were talking volubly.

"What chatterboxes you are, maids! You prattle like sparrows." This from O-Tora who entering at this moment made the sneering remark that effectually put a stop to the gay talk. As she seated herself, one of the girls, a saucy young thing, ventured to say with a demure smile. "But, Madame, women are chatterboxes by nature, aren't they? 'Nightingales visit plum-blossoms' and 'Sparrows and tigers visit bamboo grooves'; so we chattered like sparrows hoping Madame Tora (tiger) might be induced to come to us."

At this repartee the rest of the maids burst into peals of laughter and even the cross-grained duenna could not refrain from a sour smile.

"Your mention of sparrows reminds me of Takané (the name of a white-eye)" said she. "It seems the bird has not uttered a note all day. Has it been fed?"

The girls started guiltily, for so busy had they been all day they had quite forgotten to attend to the bird, a great pet with their lord who had received it, together with other gifts, from the Shogun in recognition of his military services. Nobuyuki dearly loved the bird for the sake of its song, in addition to which he prized it on account of its donor.

O-Tora, observing the consternation of the maids, revenged herself on them by saying spitefully:—

"You had better have kept your idle chattering till you had fulfilled all your duties, you good-for-nothing girls."

"It is a shame to have forgotten all about the poor little bird!" said Katsuno, who was with her companions.

"Poor thing, how hungry it must be! I will go at once and give it some food."

Stepping down into the garden, she went to an old plum-tree, and stretching up her arms took the beautifully ornamented cage of the bird off the branch on which it hung. As she did so the hook came off and the cage fell to the ground, with the result that the door came open and the little prisoner with a glad twitter escaped. With a cry of dismay the girl ran after it, but too late; the bird had already made its way through the trees and was now flying far away across the blue sky rejoicing in its freedom.

"What have you done, Katsuno?" cried O-Tora, from the verandah. Inwardly glad of this golden opportunity to carry out her dark scheme of getting Katsuno into disfavour, she yet cunningly concealed her delight under cover of fear and consternation. "Alas! You have let Takané fly away. Dear, dear, what carelessness! How could you do it!"

Katsuno, gazing up at the fast disappearing bird, seemed half stupefied. At O-Tora's words she came to herself, and then overwhelmed with thought of the consequences staggered a little and fell wailing to the ground. Her young companions standing on the verandah uttered exclamations of amazement, but none of them came to her aid, or attempted to console her. "What will you do, Katsuno?" continued the old vixen, who had by this time come down to where the unhappy girl lay, and seized her by the neck of her garment. "You know Takané is not a common bird, but a treasured present from His Highness the Shogun. Do you realize what you have done in letting it escape? Can you atone for your fault simply by a few tears? What can you do to repair the injury you have done to me, for it is I who shall be blamed,—I shall be considered responsible for this misfortune! Come, get up, girl, what have you to say?"

"Katsuno, prepare for death!" A loud and angry voice caused them all to start. Informed of what had occurred the hot-tempered Nobuyuki had rushed to the scene, and now with a drawn sword stood over the prostrate girl in a passion of ungovernable rage.

At this critical moment another voice was heard.

"My lord, my lord, wait!" It was the new Prime Councillor, Tsuda Hachiya, who thus ventured to interpose. "Calm yourself, my lord, I beg you. Do you forget the day? Is it not the holy anniversary of the demise of your revered father? Can you sully this solemn occasion with a bloody deed committed in the heat of anger? Restrain yourself and leave this matter to my discretion."

Nobuyuki's rage subsided as quickly as it had risen, and his better reason prevailed. At the remonstrance of his favourite he sheathed his sword and retired to the verandah.

By this time most of the retainers had arrived at the castle for the evening's banquet, and hearing of the incident hastened to

the scene. Shichiroyemon was among them and under cover of
the confusion whispered something to his accomplice,—then
coming forward, "How about Katsuno's chastisement, my lord?"
he said. "You act wisely in not inflicting death with your own
honourable hands, but as an apology to His Highness the
Shogun, and as an example to the clan it is necessary—it is
imperative that she should receive condign punishment."

"W-e-l-l—" Nobuyuki hesitated; then turning to Hachiya, "What
is your opinion, Hachiya? Shall I do as Shichiroyemon says?"

"No, my lord. History tells that long, long ago, in the reign of
the Emperor Takakura, one cold frosty morning, some thoughtless gardeners cut off a few branches of a beautiful maple-tree
of which the young Emperor was very fond, and burned them
to warm their *saké*. Fujiwara Nobunari, an official in charge of
the tree, greatly shocked at this, bound the offenders hand and
foot and reported the matter to the Emperor. The benevolent
monarch, however, was not enraged at all, but said calmly, "A
Chinese poet sings:—

'In woods we gathered maple-leaves*
And burned them to warm *saké*.'

I wonder how these humble gardeners have learned to have
such a refined taste? What a poetic idea!" Thus the Emperor
acquitted the careless gardeners. This is one reason why the
Emperor Takakura is revered as a great sovereign even now
after the lapse of so many centuries. So I hope and pray that my
lord who is as large-hearted as the Emperor, will be lenient with
a young girl who through no fault of her own has been so unfortunate as to cause this accident."

"Enough, Mr. Tsuda!" broke in Shichiroyemon. "You are doubtless a great scholar, and eloquent, but the slack measure you suggest would be a bad precedent. You are always tender and sympathetic with women, but in dealing with a matter such as this we
must make no distinction of sex. As well might you pardon the

---

*Lines by Hakkyoi, a great poet of ancient China.

offender who sets fire to the castle and reduces it to ashes, just because she is a woman and it was 'by mistake'! Is that justice?"

"Your argument is absurd," replied the younger man contemptuously. "You speak as if severity were a good principle in government. If so, why did Kings Chow and Chieh of ancient China, and the Tairas and the Ashikagas in our own country come to such speedy ruin? Recollect that to-day is the sacred anniversary of the demise of the father of our lord, and therefore it might well have been our lord's purpose to have set the white-eye free, himself, for the peace of the revered spirit.* The fault unintentionally committed by Katsuno has thus led to the humane act of setting a poor caged bird at liberty. I have somewhere read these lines:—

'Though one loves the sweet songs of a caged bird,
Who knows the sadness of its inner heart?'

In my opinion Katsuno has committed no fault in the true sense of the word, but on the contrary, done a good action."

With the exception of Shichiroyemon and O-Tora, all present listened with admiration to the eloquent pleading of Hachiya on behalf of Katsuno. The black-hearted pair persisted in urging the girl's expulsion from the castle, but Nobuyuki turned a deaf ear to their arguments, and decided to let the matter rest. Katsuno, all this time on her knees in the garden, now almost worshipped her deliverer in the depth of her gratitude.

III.

Tsuda Hachiya was now thirty-one. He was born the son of a farmer, but being a handsome, well-educated lad, in his sixteenth year he had been appointed to the post of page in the household of Nobuyuki who soon began to treat him with great fondness. The young samurai devoted his leisure hours to a fur-

---

*On the occasion of Buddhist funeral ceremonies, and at religious ceremonies held on the anniversary of a death, it is a common custom to set at freedom caged birds for the peace of the spirit of the deceased.

ther study of literature, and to the practice of fencing; and as he speedily evinced marked administrative ability, such as was rarely found among the intellectually ill-trained samurai of those days, he rapidly rose in the service, until now, while still a young man, he was both Prime Councillor and Steward, and exercised great authority. But notwithstanding the rank and power that might well have turned the head of one so young, he behaved modestly in public and private, and served his lord with all faithfulness and diligence, gaining thereby the admiration of the whole clan for his character and virtues.

One evening Hachiya presented himself before his lord at the latter's urgent summons.

"Hachiya," began Nobuyuki, abruptly, with a pleasant smile, "I think it is high time for you to—, isn't it?"

"Excuse me, my lord, do I not understand you?" said Hachiya with a puzzled look.

"That important affair of yours."

"That important affair of mine?" echoed the young man more puzzled than before.

"Ha, ha! how dull-witted you are to-day! The Katsuno affair!"

Hachiya did not speak. It was not the first time that Nobuyuki, who was enthusiastic over the question of Hachiya's marriage, had offered to act as middleman between him and Katsuno. Far from objecting to the proposed bride, Hachiya's inclination pointed that way, but his prudence, however, had hitherto prevailed, and he remembered the saying "a full moon is sure to wane." His appointment as Prime Councillor over the heads of older men was already calculated to give offence; should he marry Katsuno, the acknowledged beauty of the clan, would he not still further give cause for jealousy and ill-feeling? Moreover, he was not ignorant of Shichiroyemon's mad attachment, and had no desire to provoke his resentment; therefore, on various pretexts, he had month after month evaded his lord's importunity.

"Do you again say 'until next month'?" said Nobuyuki, half threateningly, as the young man remained silent. "Think not to deceive me in that way!"

Hachiya did not answer; his head was bent in respectful attention.

"Answer me at once! Still silent? . . . Tell me, do you dislike the girl?"

"Oh, no, my lord, but I fear her refusal!"

"Is that all! Set your mind at rest on that score; I have sounded her. Poor girl! Since the white-eye incident her 'sickness' has become worse and she has grown quite thin!"

Observant and sympathetic, Nobuyuki had found out that Katsuno was love-sick for Hachiya.

"Do not tease me, my lord! I will tell you of my real reasons for this hesitation."

And with this preface Hachiya gave his reasons, at each one of which the older man gave a little nod of comprehension.

"I admire your prudence and forethought," he said when Hachiya ceased speaking. "But remember you can never do anything if you think so much of the feelings of others. As for that doting old Shichiroyemon, do not fear him. I have set my heart on your happiness, and I never do things by halves. It is my wish, also, to give Katsuno the desire of her heart. But as it is so near the close of the year we will postpone the marriage till the New Year, and then I will listen to no more denials. Yes, yes, that is what we will do, Hachiya."

So saying, Nobuyuki summoned a maid and in a low voice gave an order. Presently a bottle of *saké* and some cups were brought in. Then the *fusuma* between this and the next room was gently slid open and there appeared a beautiful young woman clad in a gay *uchikaké* or gown, who knelt with movements full of grace at the threshold. It was none other than Katsuno.

"What is your pleasure, my lord?" said she bowing reverently first to Nobuyuki and then to Hachiya.

"Ah, is it Katsuno? I want you to serve us with *saké*. Sit nearer to me, Hachiya; come, let us have some *saké*."

"Excuse me, my lord. Something tells me I am needed at home; besides it is getting late. With your kind permission, I will go home at once."

"No, no; not just yet, Hachiya. Though it is late no loved one is waiting for your return, I imagine. Ha, ha! Come, you cannot refuse. Katsuno, pour him out a cup of *saké*!"

Katsuno hesitated bashfully, but on Nobuyuki's repeating his command, she took the bottle, and with a hand that trembled filled Hachiya's cup to the brim. Their eyes met and both blushed consciously.

"If you have drunk, let Katsuno have the cup," said Nobuyuki.

"I should return the cup to your lordship."

"No, I will have it after her. Give it to Katsuno."

Hachiya had no choice but to do as he was told, and accordingly offered the cup, into which he had poured more *saké*, to the maid-of-honour, who, overcome with shyness, took and sipped it with difficulty.

"Give it to me."

Nobuyuki drank off three cupfuls and then said with a sly laugh:—

"I am mightily glad you have thus exchanged the wine-cups of betrothal! Ha, ha! You have my hearty congratulations!"

The young lovers prostrated themselves in acknowledgment of his favour, but even as they did so the loud clang, clang of the alarm-bell broke the stillness of the night and caused them all to start up to listen.

"What can it be?" exclaimed Hachiya, opening the *shōji* to look out. No need to ask that question; the lurid sky, the quickly rising flames and showers of falling sparks proclaimed all too surely a house on fire!

"A fire, my lord! And not more than five *chō* beyond the pine-trees on the bank of the moat. I must go at once!"

"No doubt as to its being a fire," said Nobuyuki looking out also. "Is it not in your direction?"

"Allow me to leave your presence; I fear it is as you say!"

"Then lose no time! I will give the necessary instructions to the Fire-Commissioner myself."

With a hurried word of thanks and apology to his lord and Katsuno, Hachiya left the apartment and ran home at the top of his speed. A fierce wind had arisen and whistled through the branches of the tall old pine-trees; louder and louder clanged the iron-throated bell.

His fears were all too surely realised: he reached his home only to find it wrapped in flames! A detached room where he had been wont to study was already reduced to ashes and the fire had caught on to the main building. The trees in the garden were also burning and as the wind shook the branches they let fall a shower of sparks. A number of samurai and firemen were doing their utmost with squirts and rakes to get the fire under, but against the fierce flames fanned to fury by the strong wind their efforts were of little avail. Hachiya involuntarily heaved a deep sigh of despair, but there was no time to delay. It was imperative that he should venture into the burning building and save, if possible, important documents and ancestral treasures, as well as some highly valued gifts he had received from his lord.

As he rushed through the front gate a dark form sprang from the shade of a great pine-tree and plunged a sword into his side. Before Hachiya could draw his own weapon the assassin gave him another thrust through the heart, and the young Councillor fell lifeless to the ground.

The charred body of the hapless samurai was found in the ashes of his ruined home.

IV.

On hearing of Hachiya's death, Nobuyuki clenched his teeth, and Katsuno was beside herself with grief.

A dagger—an excellent blade by Masamuné—was found near the body. Seeing it, Nobuyuki slapped his thigh in delighted recognition, for it was a well-known weapon which his elder brother Nobunaga, Lord of Owari, had given to the elder brother of Shichiroyemon, Gemba Morimasa, one of Nobunaga's councillors. Except Morimasa nobody could have had it but Shichiroyemon; therefore, Nobuyuki who knew of the terms between his two followers, had no doubt but that his favourite councillor had fallen a victim to the jealous malignancy of the man he had superseded both in the favour of their master, and in the affection of the girl on whom he had set his heart. Added to this, a man who had been arrested on suspicion on Hachiya's premises the night of the fire, confessed after a strict examination that it was at the instigation of Shichiroyemon that he had set fire to the house.

Evidence of his guilt being so strong, some sheriffs were

despatched to Shichiroyemon's residence to arrest him; but the wily scoundrel scenting danger had fled, and it was not till after a rigorous search that it was found that he had taken refuge in the neighbouring province of Mino in the castle of Inaba, belonging to Saitō Dōzō.

O-Tora-no-Kata also disappeared about this time, and rumour had it that she was now in the mansion of Gemba Morimasa.

It was the seventh of January, and most people were enjoying the New Year festivities. But to Nobuyuki, the season brought no joy; he still brooded over Hachiya's tragic end. Buried in thought as he leant on his arm-rest, he did not notice the entrance of Katsuno, till pale and emaciated she knelt before him.

"Ah, Katsuno, I am glad to see you," he said, "I was thinking of Hachiya, and of your great grief in losing your future husband just after you had exchanged the cups of betrothal. I feel for you with all my heart!"

"Thank you, my lord," she replied sadly. "You are too good to me!"

"It is natural you should grieve," went on Nobuyuki, after a pause. "But mere sorrowing does no good to any one. Far wiser would it be to devise some way to kill the base assassin and avenge Hachiya with all speed."

"You are right, my lord,—I think my husband in Hades would be pleased to know that your lordship is willing to do so much for his honour. May I ask what is the result of your negotiations with His Excellency, the Lord of Owari?"

Nobuyuki's brother, the Lord of Owari, being the son-in-law of Saitō Dōzō, Nobuyuki had requested his brother to arrange for the delivery of Shichiroyemon, but Dōzō had ill-naturedly refused.

"This puts difficulties in our way," concluded the old lord disconsolately.

"I have a favour to ask of your lordship; may I venture to speak?"

"By all means."

"Permit me to go to Inaba, my lord."

"To Inaba! You want to go to the castle of that Saitō Dōzō?"

"Yes, my lord. I wish to enter the castle in disguise, and avenge the death of Hachiya on his murderer!"

"Not to be thought of, Katsuno!" Nobuyuki could not keep back a smile, though he saw the girl was in deadly earnest. "A young woman, and single handed!—absurd!"

"Not so, my lord, believe me!" Katsuno's eyes gleamed, and her breath came quick and fast. "I have thought it all out. I beseech you to let me go!"

Nobuyuki argued with her in vain. Her mind was made up, and nothing could shake her resolution. Therefore, he at length reluctantly gave her the desired permission, at the same time handing her the Masamuné dagger, to which reference has been made before, and saying:—

"This is the dagger with which our Hachiya was stabbed; thrust it up to the hilt in the throat of his murderer, and avenge his death!"

"I will, or die in the attempt! My lord, I thank you, farewell, fare . . ."

A burst of tears choked her utterance; she hastened from the room.

"May you have all success," said Nobuyuki, as she disappeared, and then he returned to his thoughts.

V.

In the guise of a merchant's wife, and assuming a false name, Katsuno journeyed to the castle-town of Inaba, and taking up her abode at the house of an uncle who was a farmer living in a village close to the town, watched for an opportunity to achieve her purpose.

One day, Yoshitatsu, the son of Saitō Dōzō, returning from hunting, stopped to rest at the farm-house. Katsuno waited upon him and served him with tea. Her beauty and grace of manner attracted the attention of the young nobleman. In reply to his inquiries Katsuno's uncle told him that she had recently lost her husband, a merchant, and that she was anxious to enter

the service of a daimio's lady. Yoshitatsu undertook to engage
her as maid-of-honour to his mother, and his offer was immediately accepted with joy. She was soon an inmate of the castle,
where her faithful service pleased her mistress so much that she
speedily became a great favourite.

A warm spring day, with the delicate blossoms of the cherry-
trees filling all the land with their beauty, and the faint sweetness of their perfume. Since dawn a large number of workmen
had been busily at work sweeping the courtyard of the castle,
and spreading clean sand over it. Some important function must
be on hand. Katsuno wondered what it was.

"Excuse my curiosity, my lady," she said as she served her
mistress with a cup of tea, "but for what are those men making
such great preparations? Is anything going to take place?"

"Don't you know? To-morrow there will be matches of
mounted archery."

"Mounted archery, my lady? What is that?" asked Katsuno,
feigning ignorance.

"All the samurai who are skilled in archery will practice the
art on horseback."

"Are many coming, my lady?" asked Katsuno, her heart beat-
ing high with the hope that at last she might meet her enemy.

"About a hundred, I believe, to take part in the competition,
and of course, all the samurai of our clan with their families will
be present to look on."

"Who are the archers?"

"Why do you ask?"

Katsuno was embarrassed for a moment, but quickly regain-
ing her presence of mind, she replied:—

"For no special reason, my lady; but my father, though only a
farmer, was very fond of archery, and so, from a child, I have
been interested in the sport."

"Ah, I see. Well, they brought me a programme of the day's
events this morning; here it is; you can see the names of the
archers for yourself." The lady handed Katsuno a sheet of soft,
thick paper covered with bold, black characters. With an eager-
ness she strove to conceal, she ran her eyes down the lines, till

near the middle of the page she found the name "Sakuma Shichiroyemon." At last! This was the time for which she had waited and planned.

"All the archers seem to be good samurai. What a splendid sight they will present! How I should like to see the sport, even from a distance."

"There should be no difficulty about that. You have my permission."

"My lady, I am deeply grateful." She could say no more, but such was the state of her feelings that it was with difficulty she performed her usual duties that day, nor could she sleep at all at night.

VI.

The following day the weather continued to be all that could be desired. The wide courtyard was duly prepared. The centre was enclosed for the list in the shape of an oblong square, and temporary stands had been erected all round it to accommodate the spectators; these were covered with gay carpets and soft cushions which gave colour to the scene. A dais in the very centre of the gallery on the eastern side of the lists and at a convenient distance from the target, was richly decorated with hangings of purple and white silk, which fluttered gently in the breeze. This was the place of honour for Lord Saitō and his family.

From early in the morning, samurai after samurai began to arrive at the castle, and soon every stand was crowded. The lord of the castle accompanied by his family and attended by a numerous retinue of councillors, pages, and maids-of-honour, presently appeared, and in great state seated himself in the place prepared for him. Katsuno, gaily dressed, her face powdered and painted in the usual fashion, and the Masamuné dagger concealed in the bosom of her garments, was among this company, and avoiding the attention of others, eagerly awaited her opportunity.

"To-day, or never," she thought to herself. "If I let such a golden opportunity pass, I shall never get another! Dearest Hachiya, look at me from Hades! I will avenge your death before the sun sets!" Then clasping her hands she murmured a prayer, "Oh, Hachiman, God of War, favour me with success!"

When those about to take part in the competitions were ready, the umpire, the herald, the signalman and the registrar, all betook themselves to their respective stations; a large drum being then loudly beaten to announce that the tournament was about to begin.

One after another, the archers clad in *kosodé* (silk under-clothes), *hitataré* (court robes), and *mukabaki* (breeches), came forth on horseback into the lists and rode to and fro, till coming to the appointed spot from which to aim, they shot their arrows at the mark. The judge, or umpire, would then after a careful examination give his decision, the herald would loudly proclaim the name of the archer and his achievement, while the registrar would make a written record. Then it was the part of the signal-man to announce the event to the spectators, who raised such shouts of applause that one might almost fancy the petals of the cherry blossoms fell in showers from the vibration in the air.

So archer after archer exhibited his skill, until now it was the turn of "No. 53," Sakuma Shichiroyemon. Katsuno, who had been impatiently awaiting her chance, and whose nerves were strained to the utmost, involuntarily grasped the dagger in her bosom.

Shichiroyemon rode out slowly, but as soon as he had bowed low to his lord, put spurs to his horse and dashed swiftly forward.

In her nervous excitement Katsuno pushed forward and straightening herself assumed the attitude necessary to cut at her enemy as he came up to the dais. In so doing she touched her mistress's shoulder and shrank back inadvertently, but the next moment she again pressed forward and stood ready.

Shichiroyemon galloped up with the speed of lightning, the horse's mane touched the railing of the gallery, but before the girl could act was far out of her reach.

With an exclamation of dismay she stood looking after him.

"What is the matter with you, Katsuno?" said Lady Saitō, dis-pleased at the want of manners in her favourite maid.

Recalled to herself the girl forced a laugh but replied readily enough:—

"Forgive my rudeness, my lady! In my admiration of the heroic sport I forgot myself."

"You are indeed fond of archery!"

"Yes, my lady, there is nothing I like so well."

"A strange taste for a girl!" said her mistress looking curiously at her. "But the excitement is too much for you; you are pale and your eyes are bloodshot. Have you a headache?"

"No, your ladyship, but I did not sleep last night."

"Are you not well?"

"I am quite well; it was the thought of to-day's pleasure that kept me awake."

"What a passionate lover of archery!" said the lady laughing, and Katsuno flushed at her mocking tone.

The performance of the various numbers on the programme required many of the archers to appear several times in the lists, Shichiroyemon among them. Every time he rode forth Katsuno eagerly watched for her chance, but to her intense mortification it nearly always happened that his horse was on the opposite side of the lists; and the few occasions on which he approached close enough to where she waited, he dashed past so swiftly she was unable to do anything. She wondered if her enemy had recognised her and was on his guard. She suffered an agony of impatience and fear, and almost gave up in despair.

The programme had been duly gone through, and there now remained only the final ceremony of *nanori* or "declaring of names." How would this be performed? she wondered. She feared it would not bring Shichiroyemon within her reach. Should she rush desperately into the lists and kill him there in the midst of his compeers? No, that would be too hazardous; should she fail her chance would be gone for ever. On the other hand if she let slip this opportunity was it likely she would ever get another? And she must decide quickly.

While Katsuno agonized thus, the ceremony had commenced. Each archer in his turn rode up to the dais, bowed reverentially to his liege lord, declared his name, and slowly withdrew. Quickly making up her mind she braced herself for action.

The day had advanced and it was now the middle of the afternoon. The cherry blossoms hung still in the bright sunshine, for the air had not movement enough to stir even their delicate petals. A languor seemed to have fallen on all and even the spectators showed signs of fatigue. Only Katsuno was keenly on the alert!

"No. 53!" At the call Shichiroyemon leapt on his horse, paus-
ing a moment to arrange the harness. A swift glance at him as he
sat in the full blaze of the sun showed Katsuno that he was
splendidly arrayed in a white *kosodé,* covered with a design of
nightingales perched on plum-trees. With bow and arrows in his
hand, and mounted on a snow-white steed he made a gallant
show, his bronze complexion and bushy whiskers adding to his
grim and warlike appearance. Katsuno gnashed her teeth.

After riding three times round the lists Shichiroyemon suddenly
tightened the reins and caused his horse to stop before the dais.
Then slowly riding up to the foot of the gallery he bowed low, as in
a clear voice he proclaimed his name. This moment, as he was
about to withdraw, was Katsuno's opportunity. Slipping off her
upper garment she was on the step before any one could stop her.

"Well met, Sakuma Shichiroyemon. I am the wife of Tsuda
Hachiya whom you foully murdered! Taste the sharpness of my
revenge!"

With these words she thrust the dagger into his side with all her
strength. So sudden was the attack, and such the force lent her by
desperation, that, strong man though he was, Shichiroyemon fell
forward from his saddle to the ground. With the cry "Hachiya is
avenged!" she gave him another thrust which proved mortal.

A white petal wafted by the breeze fluttered softly on to the
blood-stained dagger, and for a while all who witnessed the
scene were speechless with horror.

VII.

Saitō Dōzō, in his admiration of Katsuno's heroic deed, had it
in his mind to save the girl from the consequences of her rash
action; but as a samurai it did not accord with his honour to do
so. This for two reasons; one being that he had refused to deliver
up Shichiroyemon when asked to do so by Nobuyuki; and the
other because it was a disgrace to him personally that a warrior
under his protection should have been killed by a woman.
Therefore, he gave orders for the close confinement of the culprit, directing that she should be strictly watched and guarded
night and day.

Now that she had accomplished her long-cherished desire, and had sent word to that effect to Lord Nobuyuki, Katsuno no longer had anything to trouble her, and awaited her sentence with a tranquil mind.

One evening she was arranging some wisteria flowers which had been brought to her by one of the samurai, appointed to keep guard over her, when without any announcement Lady Saitō came into her room.

"How tastefully you have arranged those flowers, Katsuno!" she said. "Have you recovered yourself?"

The girl smiled.

"Yes, thank you, my lady; having attained my object, I have nothing left to wish for, and am ready to meet my fate."

"You are a pattern of womanhood! How I admire you! It is unbearable that one so virtuous should be subjected to the ignominy of imprisonment for so long. I have repeatedly implored my lord for your release, but as yet without avail."

"You are too good; but I have no hope of release, and I am ready to die."

"Your death would serve no end, and I do not intend to let your life be sacrificed. Listen," she came nearer and whispered in Katsuno's ear, "I have managed to get your guard sent away on some pretext, and to-night, Katsuno, you shall escape."

"Indeed, no, my lady; that cannot be! I am quite prepared for death. Without Hachiya my life is nothing to me, and should his lordship discover what you had done his wrath would be terrible,—What might he not do to you!"

"Have no fears on that point. It is not likely my lord will suspect that I had any hand in your escape, but at the worst he will not kill me. Do not think of me, but fly!"

"But my lady, . . ."

"Oh, how obstinate you are! Why will you throw your life away? Katsuno, as your mistress, I command you to escape this night!"

Seeing her mistress would take no refusal the girl gave in, and they proceeded to discuss plans.

"And when you are safe, Katsuno, how will you spend your life?"

"I shall become a nun and spend my life praying to Buddha for the peace of my dead husband's soul."

"An admirable resolve, but foolish! Have you no love for your parents?—for your family and home? Ah, forgive me, your parents and brothers are dead? I did not mean to cause you pain. But do you not see that in that case it is impossible for you to give yourself up to a life of devotion? Who then could carry on the family name?"

"But, your ladyship, I became the wife of Hachiya . . ."

"Yes, yes, but you were only betrothed! If you had married him really, the case would be different,—an engagement is nothing. No other woman would have considered it necessary to avenge his death. Your faithfulness has been demonstrated by your heroic deed. Your devotion will be handed down to posterity as a model for all wives to admire and emulate, but now that is over; other duties remain."

"What would you have me do, my lady?"

"You must marry."

"A second marriage!"

"No, a first; as you told me yourself you were never married to Hachiya, so who can blame you or call you a faithless wife if you contract a marriage with another man? Even Hachiya in the spirit world would approve of it."

Katsuno thought over these words. It was true according to the ideas in which she had been brought up that it was her duty not to let her family name die out.

"You are right," she said at length. "If I escape I will not refuse to marry." But she sighed, for her heart was with Hachiya.

"I was sure you would be sensible. And now hear what I have to say; a near relative of mine, Ōsuga Katsutaka, a retainer of Lord Tokugawa of Mikawa province, is looking for a wife. He is only twenty-seven, yet he is distinguished for his scholarship, bravery, and above all his military achievements. He has a great future before him, and, what counts with a woman before all things, he has very good looks! Will you marry him? I have already sounded him on the subject and he is anxious you should be his wife. Do not reject such a good offer."

Katsuno was silent, partly because of maiden modesty, and partly because it was too momentous a question to be decided without due consideration.

"Why do not you answer? What is your objection? I assure you that Ōsuga is every thing that can be desired; you would never regret marrying him—he is so brave and learned! But what is most important in your case, if you have two or three children by him you can adopt one of them to succeed to your father's house and carry on the family name."

"I am deeply grateful to you for all your kindness, my lady. I will do as you advise; you are wiser than I, and you know what is best."

"Then you agree? That is right, you are a good girl, Katsuno, and deserve to be happy, as I know you will be with Ōsuga. But it is getting very late and it is time you went. A palanquin is ready with ten strong footmen to convey you to the home of Ōsuga. I am sorry to part from you but it has to be, Farewell."

As she spoke, Lady Saitō handed Katsuno a letter addressed to Ōsuga Katsutaka, and a packet of money for her travelling expenses. The girl accepted them with many thanks, and bidding farewell to her mistress made her way to the postern gate from whence she safely effected her escape from the castle arriving at her destination without adventure.

VIII.

Ōsuga Katsutaka married Katsuno with the hearty approval of his lord, Tokugawa Iyeyasu, who greatly struck with admiration at the girl's heroic deed, readily promised to accord her his special protection.

On hearing of this, Shichiroyemon's brother Gemba Morimasa, a well-known warrior, who had won for himself the nickname of Gemba the Tiger, clenched his teeth in wrath and mortification, and going to his lord, Nobunaga, gave him a minute account of all that had happened, requesting him to take immediately some steps to wrest Katsuno from Iyeyasu's hand.

"If this be left undone," he continued fiercely, "my brother's spirit will never be at peace, nor will my outraged feelings allow me to rest. You must see this, my lord."

"Calm yourself, Morimasa. You speak wildly."

"Who could help it, my lord! Just think of the case! Not only was my brother murdered by a mere woman, but she, my mortal enemy, has been taken under the protection of a powerful noble, so that I am powerless to touch her! If I allow the matter to stand my reputation as a warrior will be compromised. If you decline to interfere, I will go myself and negotiate with Lord Tokugawa. At least you will allow me to do that!"

"If you are so set upon it, I will see what I can do," said Nobunaga, reluctantly; and he accordingly sent a warrior to Iyeyasu to request the delivery of Katsuno.

Iyeyasu readily granted the messenger an interview but after listening to what he had to say, replied bluntly:—

"I am sorry, but I cannot consent. Katsuno is a heroine, and such a woman as is rarely found in Japan. To speak frankly, Shichiroyemon did not behave well. I understand that because Katsuno would have nothing to say to him, and because Hachiya, to whom she was affianced, was a favourite with his lord, Shichiroyemon, out of a mean jealousy, unworthy of a samurai, caused his house to be set on fire and himself to be assassinated. In my opinion,—in the opinion of all right-minded men, he richly deserved his fate, and it was fitting he should die as he did. What can his brother urge in extenuation of his crime? His demand is preposterous! Think of Katsuno! For the sake of a man to whom she was merely betrothed, she boldly avenged his death, stabbing a strong warrior in the midst of a large concourse. What courage! It might well put a man to shame! And this heroic woman comes to me for protection, honouring me by her confidence! Do you imagine I will give her up? Never! Tell your lord that Iyeyasu is not one to betray his trust, and that he emphatically refuses to deliver up this brave woman to her enemies."

There was nothing more to be said. The messenger returned to his lord and gave the answer he had received. Nobunaga admitted its reasonableness, and not even the hot-tempered Morimasa could deny its truth. But being of a stubborn and revengeful nature, he brooded over his grievance, and secretly schemed for the attainment of his purpose.

One fine autumn day Katsuno, attended by a maid, was strolling in the grounds at the back of her residence. Sweet and beautiful she looked, with the calm happiness of a contented young wife. To the west of the garden were to be seen the quarters of her husband's retainers, and the twang of bowstrings accompanied by the whistling arrows showed that the samurai were strenuously practising their archery. A grove of maple-trees bounded the east, and their red leaves effectively contrasted with the dark green of their background. In front, to the south, the view led across paddy-fields to the tall black pines enclosing the precincts of the village shrine. A few little birds flitting here and there, and softly twittering, gave life to the scene.

Standing by a pond in the garden Katsuno was idly throwing some food to the carp which came at her call, when the little gate that gave entrance to the grounds suddenly opened, and an elderly woman came in.

"I am glad to see you, Miss Katsuno, nay, I should say Mrs. Ōsuga," said the newcomer bowing politely.

"Madame O-Tora!" exclaimed Katsuno, in surprise, quite taken aback by this unexpected visitation. "Is it indeed you? I am very glad to see you, it is long since I had that pleasure. How did you find your way here?"

"By a mere chance," replied the elder woman, smiling as though overjoyed at the meeting, and speaking in propitiatory tones. "As I was passing along this lane I happened to glance through the hedge and to my great astonishment and joy recognised you in the garden. What a happy home you have! I could envy you your good fortune!"

Katsuno made no reply to her honeyed speech, but asked curtly:—

"How do you *happen* to be in these parts? Have you come to live here?"

"That is a long story," said O-Tora in an agitated manner. "I can't tell it in a few words. I cannot stop to tell you to-day, but I will come again soon when I have more time to spare and tell you all about it. Now I must say Good-bye."

"Where are you staying?"

"Not far from here . . . but I'll come again soon . . . Good-bye!"

And she hurried away. Katsuno stood gazing after her retreating figure with an expression of mingled wonder and doubt, when suddenly from the grove of maples an arrow whizzed past and grazing her sash pierced the *shōji* of the samurai's rooms. Instantly an uproar arose, but before anything could be done another arrow whistled through the still air. Quick to think and act, Katsuno flung herself on to the ground but her maid, too much alarmed to move, stood upright where she was.

By this time the young samurai had rushed forth with loud shouts.

"The villain is hiding behind the maples," cried Katsuno. "Do not let him escape, quick, quick!"

With drawn swords the party dashed into the grove, scattering the red leaves as they pushed through.

IX.

While this was occurring, Katsuno's husband was away from home having gone up to the castle on duty. Two ruffians were caught, but unfortunately the samurai, being unacquainted with O-Tora's personality and evil intentions, did not think of trying to seize her also, though it would have been quite easy as she ran wildly hither and thither in her bewilderment and alarm.

Closely questioned, the men confessed that they were spies, and had been hired by Gemba Morimasa to assassinate Katsuno, O-Tora being decoy.

Iyeyasu, in righteous anger, caused them to be decapitated, and their heads were exposed in front of one of the castle gates with a notice which ran as follows:—

"These villains, on a strict examination, confessed that at the instigation of Sakuma Gemba Morimasa, a high retainer of Oda Nobunaga, they had come disguised to our castle-town with intent to murder. However, it may be that they were common thieves and only made up the above story to conceal their mean purposes. Therefore, we have judged them as thieves, and expose their heads accordingly."

At the failure of his plans, Morimasa flew into a terrible passion; nor could Nobunaga allow the matter to pass without notice. He despatched a messenger to Iyeyasu with a protest, to which he received the following reply:—

"If an honourable samurai of Gemba Morimasa's rank and position really intended to take his revenge on an enemy he would have come openly and in person. He would not intrust so important a task to low nameless assassins! He could not so debase his honour! This was an act worthy of a peasant, a mere tradesman, or a *rōnin*. So I concluded that those men were common thieves and in that supposition caused that notice to be written. Can Lord Oda say anything against it?"

What could Nobunaga or Morimasa urge against this temperate reply? They could not confess that the would-be murderers were indeed what they had said, and not the thieves that Iyeyasu affected to believe them. Thus were they again baffled. But Nobunaga was exceedingly enraged and determined to go to war with Iyeyasu in order to wipe out his disgrace. He diligently set about his preparations.

It was not difficult to foretell the issue of a struggle between the rival lords; Iyeyasu, with his small following, had no chance against his more powerful enemy. Katsuno was in despair. It was all through her that this danger threatened Lord Tokugawa, it was because he had refused to give her up that all this trouble had come. She had forfeited her life by her act of vengeance at the castle of Inaba, and but for the mercy of Lady Saitō she would have died long before. Though her husband loved her devotedly and she was not unhappy, still she had no desire to live, and if she were to die, there would no longer be any object in commencing a disastrous war. Therefore she would die.

In the silent watches of a winter's night when the silver moon flooded all the land with quiet beauty, Katsuno rose from her bed and with a dagger put an end to her life,—in the flower of her womanhood, at the age of twenty-two!

Katsuno left behind her four long letters addressed respectively to Iyeyasu, her husband, Katsutaka, Lady Saitō, and her former lord, Oda Nobuyuki, giving the reason for her rash act, and repeatedly thanking them for all their kindness.

A WEDDING PRESENT

A Wedding Present

"LET go! Let go, can't you!" shouted a young horseman furiously, as he raised himself up in his stirrups and angrily brandished a whip.

It was the ninth day of April in the twelfth year of Tensho (1584). The battle of Komaki Hill, one of the most important battles in Japanese history, had just been fought, and intelligence had reached the camp that Lord Ikeda Nobuteru of the Castle of Ōgaki in the province of Mino and his eldest son had both fallen. Wild with grief and rage, Terumasa, the only remaining son, had leapt upon his horse and was about to plunge headlong into the opposing lines to avenge their death when his faithful servant, Dansuké, caught hold of his bridle and with all his might strove to keep back the impetuous youth—he was barely twenty—from rushing on his fate.

But all unavailing were his remonstrances and entreaties. Quite mad for the nonce, Terumasa was determined to carry out his intention, and he struck Dansuké more than one stinging blow with his whip in order to force him to let go.

"Since you will not listen to reason, my lord, it is vain for me to seek to detain you. Go, then, and gain renown from all who shall hear of your gallant deed—friends and foes alike. I wish you good speed. Let me touch up your horse a little that he may go the faster."

With these words the man struck the horse a sound blow on the crupper; but cunning fellow that he was, he also gave the bridle a backward twist before releasing it.

Like one possessed the animal reared, and started off—not
the way his rider wished to go, but straight back in the opposite
direction.

"The devil!" cried Terumasa.

He tried to pull up; to turn round; but in vain. The horse
blessed with more sense than his master knew which way safety
lay and that way he meant to pursue. Presently, however, his
pace relaxed and Terumasa exerting all his strength managed to
arrest his flight. Patting him gently on the neck and speaking
soothing words Terumasa at length succeeded in turning him
round, and was once more on the point of performing his rash
act when once more he was stopped by Dansuké, who running
up, quite out of breath, a second time seized the bridle.

"Would you check me again, scoundrel?" shouted Terumasa.
Let go, let go, I say, or you'll repent it!"

Raising his whip again and again he brought it down each
time with telling force on the head and shoulders of the man
who dared to thwart him; but, nothing daunted, Dansuké held
on like grim death though the blood was streaming from the
cuts he received.

"My lord, my lord," he gasped. "I entreat you to be calm, and
to consider for a few moments. Of what avail is this desperate
action?"

"What, would you have me sit down quietly under this double
loss? Would you have me show myself an undutiful son as well
as a disloyal vassal? Are the vile miscreants to slay as they please
and go unpunished? Never! Let me go, I say!"

"No, no, my dear young master, I will not let you go . . . I will
not let you go thus blindly in your rage to certain death . . . What
is one man among so many? Do not think I do not understand
your feelings . . . I do, I do . . . But, my lord, when you perish in
a foolhardy, though brave, attempt to avenge the death of your
honoured father and brother, who, bethink you, will be left to
carry on the family name? . . . What will become of the noble
house of Ikeda? If you follow your relatives to Hades in this pre-
cipitate fashion, will your father be pleased? Will he commend
your devotion and say 'My son, you have done right to follow
me!' Will he not rather inquire 'In whose care have you left the

honour of our family and its concerns?' Your filial and fraternal
affection is altogether admirable, but your desire for revenge
should not blind you to the higher duty that awaits you—the
duty you owe to a long line of illustrious ancestors, the handing
on of an untarnished name . . . I do not urge that you should give
up all thoughts of vengeance only that you should postpone
their execution to a more propitious season. It is unworthy of
yourself to give way to this uncontrollable passion. Think of the
responsibility that rests upon you as the sole representative of
your family now that my honoured lord, your father, and his son
are no more. The time will surely come when you will thank me
for the restraint that so enrages you to-day. Oh, my dear young
master, do not be angry, but listen to the words of your devoted
servant.'

During this long speech Terumasa fumed and chafed, and
with kicks and blows sought to release himself. But Dansuké
would not let go his grip and earnestly did he pour forth his sup-
plication, though perforce it was delivered in rather jerky and
intermittent fashion. The bloody and tearstained countenance
of poor Dansuké at last wrought on the feelings of Terumasa
and caused him to desist. Seeing no other course open to him,
he ungraciously gave in and allowed his servant to lead his horse
back to their own camp. Here much sympathy was expressed for
him in his bereavement, but it was the unanimous opinion that
Dansuké had done right, for the time for revenge was not now
when he was only too certain to lose his own life without taking
toll of that of his enemies.

Thus did the faithful Dansuké save the life of his young master and preserve the noble family of Ikeda from extinction.

Peace reigned, for a reconciliation had been effected
between the conflicting factions of Tokugawa Iyeyasu and
Hashiba Hideyoshi, to the latter of whom the Ikedas had
adhered. Hideyoshi was proclaimed Regent. The bitter enemies
of yesterday had turned, as you turn your hand, to the warm
friends of to-day. Iyeyasu, long a widower, now sought the hand
of Hideyoshi's younger sister in marriage and was accepted.
Hideyoshi, on his side, adopted a son of Iyeyasu's for his own.

Thus "after the rain the ground hardened," as the old saying has it. All was smiling peace and goodwill between the two families which, so short a time before had been at daggers drawn, not in the figurative sense only, but in the most deadly reality.

Terumasa, his hot passion cooled down, began to look at things in a new light. To what purpose had his revered father sacrificed his life? To no purpose whatever! Not alone his father, but his elder brother and his brother-in-law—each and all had died in an utterly meaningless strife. No cause had been served by their death. By this time they were doubtless gnashing their teeth in Hades at the inconsequence of it all. He thought of his own feelings at the time and of Dansuké's devotion which had saved him from falling another victim to the fate which had overtaken his relatives.

"At the moment Dansuké said, if I recollect aright, that the time would surely come when I should thank him for restraining my rash act. Yes, he was right, though I little thought so then and only yielded because I had to. That time has come, and sooner than even Dansuké could have foreseen. He is a worthy fellow that Dansuké—I must see what I can do for him."

No sooner said than done. Terumasa, in recognition of signal service rendered in the face of danger, promoted his humble vassal to the rank of a samurai; and Dansuké, being a man of parts, once having his feet on the ladder speedily climbed to a high position. Ban Daizen, as he was now called, rose step by step till at last he reached the highest rank in the service of his lord, becoming one of the chief officials of the Bizen clan. It is within the memory of living men that on the gate of Ban's house hung a pair of rusty stirrups. These stirrups are said to have been the identical ones with which Lord Terumasa kicked the progenitor of the house, Ban Daizen, at that time plain Dansuké, under the circumstances above related, at the ever memorable battle of Komaki Hill.

Though all was peaceful between the heads of the erstwhile belligerent parties, Terumasa cherished an intense feeling of hatred towards Tokugawa Iyeyasu, and resolved never to exchange greetings with the man whom he deemed had indirectly been the cause of the death of his father and elder brother. It was inevitable that the two should meet sometimes at the palace of the Regent, and Iyeyasu was not so obtuse as not to notice the stiff attitude of the young man, and shrewd enough to guess what was passing in his mind. Having no ill will on his side, however, Iyeyasu did his best to make friends. Whenever they came across each other the older man would bow courteously and make a pleasant remark about the weather, such as "Lord Ikeda, what a fine day it is!" or "Lord Ikeda, the wind is very cold to-day!" But Terumasa was blind and deaf to all his overtures and would pass on quickly, with no acknowledgment other than a savage stare.

And thus eight years rolled on.

The Regent was well aware of the estrangement between the two great nobles, and it troubled him. He gave much thought to a plan that should alter the relations between them.

"It grieves me much," he said, one day to Iyeyasu, "to see that you and Terumasa are not on good terms. I should be glad if you were friends."

"Your Highness," replied Iyeyasu, "it is what I should like myself. The animosity is not on my side, I assure you. For what happened all those years ago at the battle of Komaki he blames me still and ever harbours thoughts of revenge. I know it from his manner, but what can I do?"

"If you will allow me, my friend, I will see what I can do for you. Let me see, you have many daughters who are, as I have been told, fair to look upon—what do you say to giving one of them in marriage to Terumasa. His wife died some time ago and he has one little son. Would you have any objection to the alliance?"

"None at all, Your Highness, but how think you? Is it likely Terumasa will listen to such a proposal? If I have any knowledge of his character he will but give a contemptuous refusal."

"Not he! Do not concern yourself on that score. I will act circumspectly, and if I am not very much mistaken, all will fall out as we desire. Will you entrust the matter to my discretion?"

"Entirely, Your Highness; and if you succeed you will have my hearty thanks."

So far, so good. Hideyoshi's next step was to summon Terumasa to his presence, and when the young man appeared, he spoke to him as follows:—

"My young friend, I hear that the sad death of your father and brother at the battle of Komaki Hill is still rankling in your heart, and that in consequence you refuse to be friends with Lord Tokugawa Iyeyasu. The occurrence was indeed lamentable but it was the fortune of war and to keep up a grudge so long against an innocent man is unreasonable. The battle was between the Tokugawas and the Toyotomis, it was no private conflict between the Tokugawas and the Ikedas. Peace has long been restored—in these days it does not become a warrior to harbour revengeful feelings against would-be friends—there are enough real foes to fight. As a personal favour to me, if for no other reason, I ask you to be reconciled to Iyeyasu and to forget the past. Or if my wish has no weight with you, for love of the Emperor and of your native land, throw off this evil feeling and be friends."

The gentle pleading of his loved chief touched Terumasa's stubborn heart. He could not say him nay.

"Your Highness," he said with his usual frank impetuosity, without giving himself time to think. "It shall be as you desire. From this moment I bid farewell to all ideas of revenge."

"Your ready compliance augurs well for your sincerity," said the great statesman, much pleased. "I thank you, dear Terumasa, and I am sure you will never regret your magnanimity."

Some more talk passed between them on indifferent subjects, but as Terumasa was about to retire the Regent seemed struck with a sudden idea.

"Terumasa," he said, "if I mistake not you are still a widower and your little son has no one to take care of him;—it is time you married again."

"Some day, Your Highness, I may think about it, but I am in no haste."

"It has just come into my head that it would be good to seal your reconciliation with Tokugawa by marrying one of his daughters. That would proclaim the fact to every one. If you permit me I will broach the matter to him."

This was going further than Terumasa altogether liked, but

seeing no help for it he gave his assent, secretly hoping the negotiations would fail.

"I leave everything to your discretion, Your Highness," he said. "I am ready to do all you wish."

"Then farewell for the present, Terumasa. I will let you know later on what success I have."

Congratulating himself on the result of his diplomacy the Regent lost no time in telling Iyeyasu. It was agreed between them that Lady Toku, the second daughter should be the bride; and Terumasa offering no objection, preparations were speedily set on foot for the formal betrothal.

But before this was celebrated, Terumasa presented himself before Hideyoshi and proffered a request.

"Since things have progressed so far by your kind mediation, Your Highness, it is of course a matter on which there can be no two opinions that my retainers become Tokugawa's and Tokugawa's retainers become mine. In a word we are reconciled and become as one family. But there is one little point that must be clearly understood. It is this. It is well known that one of Lord Tokugawa's retainers, a man named Nagai Naokatsu killed my father at the battle of Komaki. It is impossible that I should ever feel anything but enmity against this fellow. As I said before, this must be clearly understood."

The Regent was nonplussed. It were unreasonable to condemn Terumasa's sentiments on this matter, and should he do so he felt convinced that the young man would be only too glad to seize an excuse to back out of the engagement and things would go back to their old footing. Therefore, he saw nothing for it but to put a good face on the matter and to answer cordially.

"There need be no disagreement about that, my dear Terumasa. Of course you are at perfect liberty to indulge whatever feeling you like."

So the daughter of Iyeyasu was betrothed to Terumasa and it was arranged that the wedding should take place at the earliest possible date.

Towards the end of February of the next year it became necessary that Iyeyasu should go to his home in Yedo on some private business. The war with Korea was at its height and the highest military authorities had for some months been sitting in grave conclave at the Regent's headquarters at Nagoya in Hizen. Iyeyasu's presence in Yedo offered the first favourable opportunity for celebrating the nuptials of his daughter, and it was settled that Terumasa should follow his intended father-in-law to Yedo Castle as soon as possible.

Iyeyasu's thoughts as he awaited his whilom foe were not all as joyful as befitted a wedding. Anxious furrows lined his broad brow. Hideyoshi had told him what the bridegroom had said about the man who had slain those so near and dear to him, and Iyeyasu dreaded what those words might portend. The idea crossed his mind that Terumasa might even demand the head of Naokatsu as a wedding gift from the bride's father.

"See that you pay his lordship the utmost respect and honour," said he to the four chief retainers whose place it was to receive the expected guest. "It weighs heavy on my mind that he has an unconquerable animosity against poor Nagai Naokatsu. Be careful never so much as to mention his name and it may be Lord Ikeda will forget. I trust you will not fail me in this important and delicate matter."

"You may rely on our caution, my lord," answered one of those he addressed. "We will do all in our power to interest Lord Ikeda and to divert his thoughts from dangerous subjects. And for fear of accidents Nagai shall be warned to keep out of the way. Do not be anxious, my lord, we will take every precaution."

"That is well; I count on your fidelity."

In due time Terumasa arrived at the castle. Iyeyasu's four chief retainers received him with the greatest courtesy and ushering him into the spacious guest-room conducted him to the seat of honour. They then retreated backwards to the other end of the apartment, whence, with both hands on the mats, they bowed repeatedly the while they uttered words of welcome.

"Lord Ikeda, we rejoice to see you and congratulate you on your safe arrival after the dangers of your long journey. We beg to offer you our humble felicitations on the happy event that has brought you hither, and pray that all good fortune may ever attend you and your bride."

"I am glad to find myself under this roof on so agreeable a mission," replied Terumasa genially. "There is no need for me to introduce myself for you know who I am. It had been my design never to come to speaking terms with Lord Tokugawa, but through the kindly mediation of His Highness the Regent, all unfriendly thoughts have been banished and to seal our alliance I have come here this day to wed his daughter. Since the two families are to be thus united you are all my retainers, and mine are all Lord Tokugawa's. The old enmity is wiped out. We start afresh on a new and better footing. I am delighted to make your acquaintance."

"My lord, it is very condescending of you to show us so much favour. Permit us to profit by this opportunity to recommend ourselves to your good graces."

"May I enquire your names?"

"Ah, we have been remiss! I, who speak, am Ii Naomasa, at your service."

"And I am Sakai Saemon, your lordship."

"Can it be! I know your names well and I recall seeing you both at a distance now and again before your camp at the time of the battle of Komaki Hill. Yes, you fought valiantly."

"Your lordship flatters us. We do not deserve such praise."

"And who may you be, my friend?"

"My name, your lordship, is Nakatsukasa Tadakatsu, formerly Honda Heihachiro."

"I know, I know! It was a misty morning when I saw you fighting bravely on the bank of the river near Ryūsenji Temple in Kasugai. Yes, yes, you, too, acquitted yourself splendidly."

"My lord, I do not merit such commendation; I am but a plain soldier."

"There is one more—may I ask your name also?"

"Sakakibara Yasumasa, my lord."

"Do I behold the countenance of the renowned Sakakibara?—Sakakibara, who by himself gave chase to Lord Hideyoshi when he was forced to retreat near Hosonigaki? Your temerity on that occasion is still vividly remembered by His Highness. He admits, of an evening when in a talkative mood, that he was never so terrified in his life! Ha, ha, ha! You were a bold man."

"The past is past and forgotten, my lord. I am now one of the most faithful and obedient servants of His Highness. We whose trade is that of arms, fight and make peace as the god of war casts his dice—we have no choice in the matter."

"The presence of so many brave soldiers who took part in the battle of Komaki Hill gives me much pleasure. My thoughts are carried back to the past and—that reminds me—my brave sirs, will you answer me one question?"

"As many as it is your pleasure to put, your lordship."

"I have heard of one Nagai Naokatsu who was also at the battle; what has become of him?"

This was a bolt from the blue! The four veterans, brave men though they were, looked from one to the other in consternation and dismay, quite at a loss how to reply. That which their lord had warned them against had befallen in the very first hour. Terumasa seeing, and it must be confessed, enjoying, their discomfiture, pressed for his answer.

"What has become of Nagai? Where is he now?" he repeated, impatiently.

Another exchange of glances. Not one of them dared to take upon himself the onus of the answer.

"Have you suddenly lost your hearing, sirs? I ask again, What has become of Nagai?"

It was plain that Terumasa was losing his temper.

"Begging your lordship's pardon," faltered Sakai Saemon, behind whom the others were gradually insinuating themselves as they pushed him forward to fulfil his usual office of spokesman, "I believe he is in good health, and still in our lord's service."

"Still in your lord's service? I am glad of that; it removes a great weight from my mind. It is to see this same Nagai, the murderer of my father, that I have covered so many miles. You will oblige me by bringing him before me without delay."

"My lord, I venture to suggest that you send for him after your interview with Lord Tokugawa."

"That can wait. I desire to see this Nagai first. If you refuse, it only remains for me to leave Yedo at once without paying my respects to his lordship. I have spoken."

There was no doubting that Terumasa meant what he said. There was nothing for it but to apprise their master of what had happened in spite of their precautions, and to leave the matter to his judgment. Sakai Saemon bowed low as he said:—

"My lord, deign to wait a few minutes. I will oblige you with all speed."

"No equivocation, mind. Beware how you play with me!"

Sakai withdrew, his three friends having already disappeared. Terumasa smiled grimly to himself. Nothing was lost upon him.

The four retainers hastened to their lord's chamber. He looked up as they entered and asked pleasantly:—

"Well, he has arrived?"

"Yes, your lordship."

"Is all well?"

"No, your lordship; we fear the worst has happened."

"How! What do you mean?"

"He demands to be at once confronted with Nagai."

"Did I not warn you . . ." began Iyeyasu, angrily; then he checked himself, and with arms folded and head sunk on his breast, considered the situation.

"You say that Lord Ikeda insists on seeing Nagai Naokatsu at once?" he queried presently, looking up.

"Yes, your lordship."

"Then by all means, let him see Nagai. Lord Ikeda is not a madman. He has come here to marry my daughter. It is not likely, unless he is out of his mind, that he will upset all our plans and imperil the favour of the Regent just to satisfy an old grudge."

"Judging from his words and manner there is no saying what he may or may not do, your lordship."

"Humph!"

"Should he put his hand on his sword when he finds Nagai before him, we shall not be able to stop him from wreaking his vengeance. Or should he demand Nagai's head for a wedding present, how can we refuse?"

"Will he go so far as that?"

"Nothing more likely, your lordship."

"I was afraid of this. Let me think what can be done."

Iyeyasu pondered awhile, a deep frown of perplexity and trouble on his forehead. Then as if a solution had suddenly come to him his eyes sparkled, and he spoke firmly.

"Take Nagai Naokatsu into the presence of Lord Ikeda as he desires, and if he demands his head as a wedding gift deny him resolutely. Those are my orders."

"Your lordship, it is easy to obey, but if we act like that there will be an end to the proposed marriage, and you will incur the displeasure of His Highness, the Regent. Dare you run such a risk?"

"Do not trouble yourselves about results, only do as I tell you. If Lord Ikeda asks for the head of Nagai as a wedding gift, remind him that the battle of Komaki was fought between the Tokugawas and the Toyotomis—it was no private affair of the Ikedas. Nagai served under his chief and killed General Ikeda Nobuteru by the fortune of war. It was one of the chances of battle and in a fair field. Nagai did but do his duty. If Terumasa feels any animosity for the death of his relatives it should be directed against me, the principal, not against Nagai who was only fighting under my orders. Therefore, tell him, he is welcome to wreak all his vengeance upon my daughter, Lady Toku, his bride. Let him cut her in strips if so he wills and I shall not interfere, but let him understand explicitly that Iyeyasu will never sacrifice his loyal retainer on any consideration whatever."

"My lord, your words impress us deeply. We will return and try to adjust the matter to the satisfaction of all parties!"

Nagai Naokatsu was sent for. The four retainers told him how things stood, and further instructed him to be on his guard, ready to fly should the young nobleman's hand move towards his sword-hilt.

Then the four went back to the guest-room where Terumasa fuming and chafing had been waiting all this time.

And now it was Sakakibara Yasumasa who spoke first.

"My lord, we apologize for the long delay," he began.

"Have you brought Nagai—where is he?" Terumasa interrupted him.

"Yes, my lord, he is without."

"That is well. Show him instantly into my presence."

"Yes, my lord."

The sliding screens were pushed aside and there, in the antechamber, at a very respectful distance calculated for the convenience of making his escape in case of need, sat Nagai, his bent head hiding his face.

"Are you Nagai?"

"Yes, your lordship."

"Come here, Nagai."

"My lord, I am unworthy to approach your honourable lordship."

"Away with excuses! Come here, I say."

"My lord, I cannot venture so far."

"You try my patience beyond its limit, sirrah!"

Terumasa rose to his feet precipitately and crossed the intervening space to where Nagai crouched. The sweat burst out on the four men who were witnesses of the scene; they trembled for what would come.

"Why do you not come when I call?" thundered Terumasa, seizing the other's wrists and dragging him over the floor. "I'll teach you to obey at once!"

Terumasa being a big man and possessed of great strength, Nagai was as a sparrow in the talons of a hawk and entirely at his mercy. Before he had time to think, much less struggle, he found himself landed by the cushion where Terumasa had been sitting since his arrival and on which he again seated himself.

"Look at me, sirrah!" commanded Terumasa.

"My lord," said the frightened wretch, "I cannot do that."

"Look at me. You were not such a craven when you killed my father Nobuteru in cold blood, on the ninth day of the fourth month in the twelfth year of Tensho."

"All the more reason why I should quail now, your lordship."

"You are a most obstinate fellow! Why will you never do as I tell you?"

Terumasa took hold of the man's collar and twisted his face upwards. Looking calmly and critically at it for a moment or two he observed complacently.

"Well, Nagai Naokatsu, it affords me much gratification to look at you. I have been told that you have the best appearance of all the men in the service of Lord Tokugawa. My informant was right—you are undoubtedly a very handsome man, though at the present moment you do not appear to the best advantage . . . It is a satisfaction to know that my father met his death at the hands of so creditable a soldier. Without doubt he went the less reluctantly to the spirit world. So far, well, Nagai."

Naokatsu gave himself up for lost. Though far from being a coward at ordinary times, the stern aspect and speech of Terumasa whom he had so greatly, though inadvertently, wronged, awed and intimidated him.

The four retainers stood prepared to interfere at the last moment should it be necessary, and they too thought Nagai's doom was sealed.

Still keeping his grip on the collar of his victim's garment, Terumasa continued to gaze at him thoughtfully. Then turning to the other men he asked abruptly:—

"What annual stipend does he receive at the present time?"

"One thousand *koku*° of rice from his fief near Kawagoé."

"And how much did he get at the time of the battle of Komaki?"

"Two hundred *koku*, your lordship."

Terumasa flung the man from him and clapped both hands on his knees. Tears of mortification stood in his eyes.

"Can I credit my ears? At the time of the battle his stipend was two hundred *koku*; now after the lapse of well-nigh ten years it has risen to only one thousand *koku*, and that derived from an out-of-the-way hole like Kawagoé! Ah, what a worthless fellow he must be! To think that my revered father perished by the hand of such an insignificant creature! It is too humiliating!

°A *koku* is about four bushels; in feudal days it was customary to pay the samurai in rice.

Father, I fear you can never forgive yourself for allowing such a disgraceful thing to happen. You must everlastingly be bemoaning your untoward fate in the land of the shades. I, Terumasa, your son, sympathise with you from the bottom of my heart!"

His emotion was so genuine that tears trickled down his dark cheeks and he seemed to forget that there were witnesses of his unusual weakness. Not for long, however. Recovering his composure, he turned his eyes on the men before him.

"Sirs," he said, "I told you a short time since, that my main object in coming to Yedo was to behold the countenance of this man, the slayer of my father and brother. I have seen him and am not disappointed. But there is one request that I desire you will kindly submit to my future father-in-law. It concerns this same Nagai Naokatsu. If, according to custom, his lordship intends giving me a wedding present. . . ."

Here it was at last! The four chief retainers could not restrain a shudder, and the face of Nagai grew livid. It was Ii who first found his voice.

"My lord," he stammered, "what you say is reasonable and we expected as much. But will you not let bygones be bygones? The Komaki affair happened nearly ten years ago and it is too late to rake it up. Moreover, this is a day highly blessed by the god of peace—a day on which two noble families are to be joined. Let not such an occasion be marred by a deed of revenge and blood. I entreat your lordship to reconsider your words and mercifully to let Nagai live!"

"My lord, we all unite in humbly pleading for the life of this unfortunate man!" chorused the other three, as all threw themselves down with heads touching the mats before him.

"What are you all talking about?" said Terumasa, unceremoniously. "Who said I wanted the life of Nagai? Nothing is further from my thoughts. This is what I wish you to ask Lord Tokugawa—that he will use his influence with His Highness, the Regent, to have this fellow created a daimio, as soon as possible, with an annual income of, say, ten thousand *koku*."

Amazement was depicted on the faces of the five men—amazement and relief. Iyeyasu, who behind a sliding screen had heard all that had passed, now pushed it aside and ran into the room. Clasping Terumasa's hands in his he raised them to his head while he gave vent to his feelings as follows:—

"Terumasa, you have acquitted yourself nobly! I am unworthy of so magnanimous a son-in-law. What can I say but that I will do all in my power to further your truly chivalrous request."

After the wedding Terumasa returned with his bride to the city of Nagoya, where Iyeyasu soon followed him. He told the whole story to the Regent and proffered his request. Hideyoshi slapped his knee in approval.

"Terumasa is a true samurai," he said. "Rest assured his petition shall meet with immediate attention."

Accordingly, Nagai Naokatsu, a minor vassal, of one thousand *koku*, from a place near Kawagoé, was at a bound promoted to the dignity of a daimio worth ten thousand *koku* yearly.

So you see that Ikeda Nobuteru did not fall by the sword of a nameless samurai!

THE HEROISM OF
TORII KATSUTAKA

The Heroism of Torii Katsutaka

THE little garrison besieged in the Castle of Nagashino, in the province of Mikawa, was in desperate straits.

Okudaira Sadayoshi, Governor of the castle, was away at a distance on business of importance, and his son, Sadamasa, was left in command with a small company of but eight hundred men. These fought with the courage of despair; but having been taken at unawares, the castle was ill provided with ammunition and provisions, and at the end of a fortnight death, from starvation, or the alternative of surrender, stared them in the face.

It was at the close of April in the third year of Tensho (1575). Takeda Katsuyori, Lord of Kai, knowing his feudal enemy, Sadayoshi, to be absent, deemed it a good opportunity to attack his stronghold; and, therefore, at the head of 28,000, suddenly swooped down and surrounded the castle. Stationing his headquarters on a hill opposite the main entrance, he invested it on all sides, day and night continuing the assaults on the walls, so that, if possible, it might fall into this hands before either Sadayoshi's liege lord, Tokugawa Iyeyasu, or the latter's powerful ally, Oda Nobunaga, could come to the rescue.

By the end of two weeks some three hundred of the defenders had been killed, or so seriously wounded as to be incapable of rendering further aid; and sparing though they had been of it, food remained for barely two days more. In this sore strait Sadamasa summoned all his men and with calm courage and determination addressed them as follows:—

"My men," he said, "I cannot speak too highly of your bravery

69

and devotion, and I thank you. But the odds against us are too great and the castle must be given up. Our ammunition has almost run out and we have food for but two days more. To send for help is impossible, so closely does the enemy watch every outlet. I will send an envoy to Takeda requesting that you may all depart unmolested, while I myself will commit *seppuku*. It may be in your hearts to fight to the end rather than surrender the castle, but of what avail would it be for you thus to sacrifice your lives. It would do no good to me nor to anyone else. It is my wish that you should all live to join my father and hereafter fight again for him and it may be recover the castle that we are now forced by wholly unforeseen and unavoidable circumstances to yield. There is nothing else to be done. Save yourselves and allow me to commit *seppuku*."

Sadamasa ceased speaking, but before the sound of his grave tones had died away, a ringing voice from the rear took up his words.

"Commit *seppuku*, my lord! It is too soon to talk of such a desperate measure! With your permission I will steal my way through the enemy's lines and summon reinforcements before it is too late."

"Is it Katsutaka who speaks? My brave fellow, I appreciate your desire, but the idea is quite impracticable. How could a rat, much less a giant like you over six feet, get through the enemy's lines unobserved, and supposing such a miracle accomplished, how could an army reach us in time to avert our dying from starvation? It is not without deep consideration that I have come to the conclusion that I have just made known to you. Your project is impossible."

"Not so, my lord," Katsutaka spoke quietly like a man who has fully made up his mind and knows what he is about. "As you know, I am a good swimmer, and I am strong. I will cross the river in the dark and hurrying at utmost speed to His Excellency Lord Tokugawa lay before him our need and request the instant despatch of troops to disperse the besiegers. I have thought the matter over; I can do it."

"Bravely conceived and bravely spoken, Katsutaka! Well, desperate diseases call for desperate remedies. You can but fail and we shall be no worse off than before. Go, my friend, and may luck attend you!" He paused, for emotion made it difficult to speak; then recovering his voice, he went on:—"Should you effect your escape, as you hope, it is necessary that we should know of it that we may hold out to the last minute. How can you inform us of the fact!"

"Easily, my lord. I will climb to the summit of Mt. Funatsuki and cause smoke to rise by way of a signal. From thence to Okazaki where Lord Tokugawa is in residence is a distance of only twenty-three miles or so. I shall arrive at his castle by noon to-morrow, and having delivered my message shall return without delay."

"And how can you tell us of the coming of reinforcements?"

"At midnight, the day after to-morrow, I shall be back on the mountain, and again I will signal to you by smoke. One column of smoke will mean that His Excellency Lord Tokugawa's troops are coming alone; two will mean that they are accompanied by those of Lord Oda; and three will signify that His Excellency's army has been joined by both Lords Oda,—an allied army of three divisions."

"Can you by any possibility inform us of the number of troops?"

"Nothing easier, my lord. One shot will tell you that 10,000 troops are on their way; two shots, 20,000; three shots, 30,000. Have no fears, my lord. I am confident that I shall succeed."

"Heaven aid your heroic spirit, Katsutaka! When do you propose to start?"

"With your permission, as soon as it is dark, my lord. There is no time to be lost. Farewell!"

"Stay, my friend. I will give you something before you go. See here."

Katsutaka approached nearer and his master gave into his hands a case of costly incense and a valuable sword.

"This incense is a family treasure, having been handed down from our ancestor, Prince Tomohira, the seventh son of the Emperor Murakami; and this sword is another heirloom—a noted blade by Sadamunĕ. Take these articles as some small recognition of your bravery and loyalty."

With deep reverence the soldier received the precious gifts.

"Your lordship is too good to his humble servant. I accept your generosity with profound gratitude."

"Stay yet again, Katsutaka! I must pledge you in a parting cup."

Two cups were brought and a bottle of *saké*. Katsutaka then executed a war-dance singing a martial strain the while. Then he departed to make the few preparations necessary for his perilous undertaking, leaving all those assembled, both officers and men, full of admiration for his heroism.

Clad in the lightest attire and with a small packet wrapped in waterproof oil-paper in his hand, in the stillness of night, Katsutaka stole out of a postern gate and crept to the bank of the River Iwashiro which flowed at no great distance past the castle. The rainy season having already set in, the stream was much swollen and the swift current in its windings dashed furiously against either bank in turn. Katsutaka hid himself among the tall reeds growing on the edge and cast a searching eye in every direction. The full moon, breaking out of a heavy bank of clouds, made the night almost as bright as day; and to his dismay the adventurer saw that a web of large and small ropes to which were fastened innumerable clappers was extended over the stream, and that a close line of sentinels was on guard on the opposite shore. When anything happened to touch the ropes the clappers would rattle loudly "gara-gara, gara-gara," and at each rattle the sentinels were on the alert with torches to discover the cause of the noise.

At this unexpected difficulty Katsutaka was greatly taken aback. How could he swim across the river in the face of such vigilant precautions? To add to his dismay he saw waving lazily in the gentle night breeze an *umajirushi* or "horse-badge" and a flag, both bearing a coat of arms that he knew belonged to Baba Nobufusa who was esteemed the ablest of all the veteran generals of the opposing army.

"I am certainly under an unlucky star," groaned Katsutaka. "With Baba Nobufusa in charge of this side it is well-nigh impossible for me to cross the river and effect a landing. But I will not give up without doing my best, and it may be I shall yet find a way to elude their vigilance."

He tore up a reed and was about to hurl it into the river when

"May I ask you to explain the place of honour given to a garden *geta*?"
(*Ungo-Zenji*, p. 9)

"I caught these sparrows quite of my own accord." (*The Loyalty of a Boy Samurai*, p. 19)

She filled Hachiya's cup to the brim. (*Katsuno's Revenge*, p. 32)

Terumas took hold of the man's collar and twisted his face upwards. (*A Wedding Present*, p. 64)

He raised his voice so that every word rang clear and distinct.
(*The Heroism of Torii Katsutaka,* p. 81)

Gonshiro threw him by a supreme effort down on the mats. (*The Wrestling of a Daimio*, p. 90)

"A warrior burns incense into his helmet when he is determined to die on the field." (*The Story of Kimura Shigenari*, p. 114)

"Whose hat is that?" (*Honest Kyusuke*, p. 127)

it struck him that if the root had earth on it the sagacious Nobufusa would conclude that some one was hiding in the vicinity and order his soldiers to make a strict search. That would be fatal to his enterprise. He, therefore, washed the mud off the reed and then threw it into the stream. Immediately it got entangled in the network of ropes and set all the clappers clattering loudly, "gara-gara, gara-gara."

On the instant two sentinels leapt into the water and drew the reed to land. It was taken to Nobufusa who carefully examined the root by the light of a torch.

"There is nothing suspicious about this reed," said the general. "It is of no consequence."

Katsutaka, peering intently from his hiding place on the other side, felt his heart sink.

"It is hopeless to think of crossing," he said to himself.

After a few moments of despondency he once more uprooted a reed and washing off the mud as before cast it into the river. Again the clappers were set a-going and again some of the men plunged into the water to seek the cause.

"Another reed, my lord," said the man who handed it to the general.

"The reeds are being washed off the bank by the flood," he remarked after examining the reed. "It is nothing; but nevertheless do not relax your vigilance, my men."

Katsutaka now picked up a dead branch that had been washed ashore, and threw it at the ropes, and after that another reed. So he went on, throwing now one thing, now another, keeping the clappers rattling so unintermittingly that in time Nobufusa's soldiers ceased to take notice of the sound and no longer dashed into the river at every fresh repetition. Still, however, Katsutaka could not venture to enter the river himself, for watchful eyes never left off scanning the dark waters. Time was passing. What could he do? Katsutaka was well-nigh in despair. To return and confess he had failed at the very outset was insupportable—unthinkable even!

Just then he heard the roll of a drum—the guard was being relieved. Nobufusa's men retired and Atobé Ōinosuké's took their place.

Katsutaka's spirits rose. Ōinosuké was noted for his subtlety, he knew, but could not be compared with Nobufusa in patient strategy. Once more Katsutaka began throwing things into the river, but the fresh sentinels were very much on the alert and examined everything that set the clappers rattling. Poor Katsutaka was feeling indeed hopeless when the heavy clouds that had been coming up unobserved, obscured the moon and there was a low rumble of thunder in the distance. Then with appalling swiftness the storm was upon them. The noise was terrific. The heavy rush of the rain that came down in sheets, the roar of the wind and the roll and rattle of thunder made a pandemonium of the erstwhile peaceful night.

Katsutaka had no fear of the elements; he only thought that now his course was clear. He danced and shouted for joy, knowing that he could be neither seen nor heard through the tumult and pitchy darkness. But no time was to be lost. The storm might pass over as rapidly as it had come. Stripping himself bare and tying his oil-paper package round his neck he slipped into the turbid waters and with his dagger cut some of the ropes that crossed it. The noisy clappers sounded faintly to the watchers on the opposite bank, but as some men were about to investigate their general stopped them.

"It is unnecessary, my men," he said. "The clappers are moved by fish coming down the flood from the upper reaches of the river. None of the garrison opposite would be so mad as to attempt to cross in such a storm—it would mean instant death. Therefore be reassured."

"You speak truly, my lord," asserted one of the men. "It can only be fish as your honour says."

Tossed and whirled about by the current, Katsutaka struggled to the opposite bank at a point about half a mile from where he had started. He found this part also well guarded, but hoped that under cover of the darkness and noise he might get through. Stealthily he was making his way when suddenly his foot slipped on the wet ground and he fell with a slight thud.

"Who goes there?" rang out the quick challenge in his ear.

Startled, Katsutaka scrambled to his feet and laid his hand on the hilt of his dagger.

"One of the patrol, sir," he answered readily.

"Is that all? I pity you out in the storm. Pass on!"

"Thank you, Captain. Good-night, sir."

"Good-night. Do not relax your care. The enemy may take advantage of the storm."

"I will take care, sir."

Thus his presence of mind saved the situation when all seemed lost, and the first and most difficult part of his enterprise was accomplished.

By the time Katsutaka had ascended to the summit of the mountain from whence he intended to signal, the rain had almost ceased and the rumble of thunder was barely audible in the growing distance. As he paused to take breath the moon shone out again and bathed the landscape in silvery loveliness. With material brought in his little package he managed to make a small blaze, trusting it would be seen by the watchers at the castle who would be anxious to know of his escape. Then once more resuming his journey he hastened down the declivity and with no further adventure arrived at the town of Okazaki about 10 o'clock the following morning.

As he drew near the castle he met an officer on horseback attended by a few men on foot. To his great joy he recognized his own chief, Lord Okudaira Sadayoshi. Placing himself in the way and bowing with due reverence,

"I am Torii Katsutaka, my lord," he said, "and I have come on an urgent errand from your honourable son at present beleaguered in the Castle of Nagashino."

"Beleaguered! My son beleaguered! What mean you by such strange tidings? Follow me; I will return to the castle instantly."

Turning his horse and followed closely by his retinue and Katsutaka, Sadayoshi cantered quickly back the way he had come and dismounting in the courtyard demanded of the messenger a more explicit and detailed account of how matters stood. He was indignant beyond measure at what he heard.

"This is wholly unexpected and unwelcome news," he exclaimed. "My brave fellow, your daring deed is beyond all praise. I came here two days ago with Lord Tokugawa, on my way home intending to stay a short time. Now I must proceed instantly. Wait here while I go to tell His Excellency; it may be he will wish to question you himself."

In a very short time an attendant summoned Katsutaka to the presence of the famous statesman.

"Torii Katsutaka," said he kindly, "you are a brave man, and have done a wonderful thing. Let me know exactly how matters stand at the Castle of Nagashino. You have my permission to speak to me directly."

Expressing his sense of the honour shown him, Katsutaka, in the simple words of a plain soldier, gave a detailed account of the state of affairs within and without the castle when he had left it.

"If reinforcements be not instantly despatched, Your Excellency," he concluded, "the garrison will starve to death. I entreat, Your Excellency, let no time be lost."

"Reinforcements shall be sent with all possible speed," said Iyeyasu. "By a happy chance both Lords Oda are now in this province with their troops, and they can reach the besieged castle in two, or at the most, three days. But for you we should have known nothing till too late. You are a hero indeed. Now go and get food and rest before you start on your return journey."

The afternoon of the same day, Iyeyasu, at the head of 20,000 men, proceeded to the castle of Ushikubo, where he was joined by the two Lords Oda with their combined forces of 50,000 men. Arrangements were set on foot for an early start the next morning.

Iyeyasu then spoke to Katsutaka again:—

"As you see, our allied armies will be able to reach Nagashino in two days at the latest. So rest assured that the relief will be in time. You must be greatly fatigued. Remain here a few days till you are fully rested."

"Your Excellency is too considerate, but I cannot take advantage of your kindness. I must return at once and tell the garrison of the success of my mission and that help is coming. Allow me to set out without delay."

"By your own showing it would be quite impossible for you to re-enter the castle in the manner in which you came out. Do not be rash, but stay here as I advise you."

"A thousand pardons, Your Excellency," said Katsutaka, respectfully, but firmly. "At the risk of my life I undertook this errand; I will carry it through to the end. It is an honour more than my poor life is worth to have been granted speech with Your Excellency and favoured with words of commendation from your august lips. Life can offer me no higher grace. Even should I be captured by the enemy and put to an ignominious death I should have nothing to regret. The garrison is starving; to know that help is on the way will give them new life. Permit me to go, Your Excellency."

"If you are so set upon it," replied Lord Tokugawa, "I will say no more. You shall take a letter from me to Sadamasa."

"That would be dangerous, Your Excellency. If the letter were found on my person notice would be given of your approach and the enemy would take steps accordingly."

"Right," said Iyeyasu with a smile. "You are wise as well as brave, my Katsutaka!"

Then Katsutaka bade farewell to Lord Tokugawa and Lord Okudaira Sadayoshi, and shouldering his gun set out once more on his perilous journey.

Anxiously did the diminishing and weakened garrison at the besieged castle wait for the signal that should tell them help was coming. Cheered by the knowledge that Katsutaka, contrary to expectation, had succeeded in eluding the sentinels they now had some hope that he would have the same good fortune in his further quest. In turn watchmen went up to the high tower and strained their eyes in the direction whence the promised signal would appear. At midnight of the second day, to their boundless joy, they descried a light as of a bonfire on Mt. Funatsuki; and soon three columns of dark smoke rose in the still air plainly seen against the sky that was lighted up by a great round moon. Help was coming! But would it be sufficient? How many troops were on their way? Hark! a sharp report, and then another and yet another till seven shots gave the glad assurance of the approach of 70,000 men. The starving men took heart again, and forgetting hunger and wounds looked forward with joy to their speedy relief.

But the sound of the shots reached other ears as well as those for which it was intended. The company on guard at the foot of the mountain heard it too, and a detachment went up to investigate. General Naito Masatoyo himself led the little band. With no thought of danger Katsutaka, triumphant, was gaily running down when he found himself surrounded by the very men he wished to avoid.

"Halt! Who are you?" demanded the general.

Katsutaka's ready wit did not desert him.

"Hearing shots, I have been with my comrades to find out what they meant. We have searched everywhere but can find no one. I am coming down to report our failure."

"Come nearer and let me see your face. Who is your captain?"

"I belong to the company of riflemen under the command of Captain Anayama."

"Your name!"

"My name—my name is . . ."

"Men, take this fellow prisoner."

More easily said than done. At the command four or five soldiers sprang forward to obey, but Katsutaka made such a vigorous defence that they found it impossible to hold him; and freeing himself from their grasp he ran down towards the foot of the hill. More soldiers were coming up, however, so he turned back, hoping under cover of some bushes to slip past and thus escape. But he was seen and caught as in a trap. Dealing heavy blows right and left he made a good fight, but the odds were too overwhelming and he was at last forced to yield. His gun was taken from him and handed to the general who found thereon an inscription in red lacquer, "One of 3,000 guns belonging to the Castle of Okazaki."

The truth flashed upon him. He guessed that the man they had captured had been to Okazaki to ask for reinforcements. Late though it was he must be taken before the Commander-in-chief, General Katsuyori, at once.

Bloodstained and travel-worn Katsutaka presented a pitiable sight when, roused from his slumbers, the general surveyed him by the imperfect light of a lantern. Yet there was something in the bearing of the man that called forth a feeling of admiration for his courage rather than compassion for his condition and circumstances.

"Your name?" said the general.

Having no motive now for concealment Katsutaka spoke out boldly.

"Torii Katsutaka, retainer of Lord Okudaira Sadamasa, Governor of the Castle of Nagashino."

"You have been to Okazaki, for reinforcements, and fired those shots from the top of Mt. Funatsuki by a prearranged plan. Is it not so?"

"It is so, Your Excellency."

"It was a hazardous errand. You must tell me later how you managed to creep through our lines. I know how to appreciate and reward bravery, and would like to number you among my men. If you will come over to us I will give you a yearly stipend of 1,000 *koku* of rice. If you refuse you die."

Pretending to be pleased with the offer Katsutaka accepted it with many expressions of gratitude. He was thinking that by doing this he might put his captors off their guard and be able to escape, or in some way render a service to those shut up in the castle.

"You do me too much honour, Your Excellency," he said. "I am but a humble private but I will use all diligence to serve you faithfully."

"I am glad you are troubled by no foolish scruples as to desertion," said the general, who nevertheless was somewhat surprised at the ready acceptance of his proposal. "There is something I desire you to do at once to prove your sincerity."

In a low voice General Katsuyori gave an order to an *aide-de-camp*, who retired and after a little time came back with a written paper which he handed to his chief. It purported to be a letter from Sadayoshi to his son, informing him that, on account of a sudden outbreak of insurrection, Lord Tokugawa was unable to despatch troops to the relief of the Castle of Nagashino and that there was nothing to be done but to give it up on the best terms available. The letter was a skilful imitation of Sadayoshi's hand, for it had been written by an officer who had once served under him and who was well acquainted with his style.

Showing the forgery to Katsutaka with no little pride, Katsuyori said:—

"Now, my man, you must write another letter to confirm the intelligence contained in this one, and both letters shall be at once shot over the walls. What! do you hesitate?"

Seeing no course open to him but to obey, Katsutaka did as required. The two missives were then fastened to an arrow and shot into the castle by a skilled archer.

The consternation and disappointment of the expectant garrison can be better imagined than described. All the more bitter was this news from the hope that had preceded it. Strong men wept.

But Okudaira Jiyemon, chief Councillor, having closely examined the letters, burst out laughing.

"It is hardly an occasion for mirth, Jiyemon," said Sadamasa, much displeased at this untimely merriment. "May I inquire the nature of the joke?"

"Ha, ha, ha! I beg your lordship's pardon, but Katsuyori is a dull fellow to imagine we could be taken in so easily. Be so good as to look at this paper—it is not the kind manufactured in this province such as our lord always uses, but in theirs. That one fact gives them away. Never fear, my lord! Take my word for it, Katsutaka's signals told the truth. This is but a plot to deceive us into surrendering before help comes."

It was now plain to all that the letters were not genuine and their spirits again arose. Going up to the high tower Sadamasa called so that the sentinels on the other side could hear him.

"Soldiers of Kai, approach! I have something to say in answer to the letters sent me but now. Request an officer to come near enough to hear my words."

Nothing doubting but that Sadamasa wished to make terms of surrender, Katsuyori himself came forth, attended by his suite.

"Accept my best thanks for your arrow-letters," began Sadamasa politely. "It was good of you to pass on my father's communication and I am much obliged to you." Then suddenly changing his tone, "Do you think," he thundered, "that such a clumsy trick could deceive us or induce me to give up the stronghold of my ancestors? Fools! The laugh is on our side! Ha, ha, ha!"

"Ha, ha, ha!" roared the men behind him greatly enjoying the discomfiture of the men below.

Katsuyori was furious.

"Go, Katsutaka," he shouted. "Go to the edge of the moat and tell them that no reinforcements are coming—that they must surrender!"

Guarded by two men, for he had not yet been set at liberty, Katsutaka stepped forward to the edge of the moat, and raising his voice so that every word rang clear and distinct,

"Listen, my lord, and comrades," he said. "What I tell you is the truth. Lord Tokugawa and the two Lords Oda, with an allied army of 70,000 men are hastening to your rescue. They will be here to-morrow without fail. The arrow-letters are utterly false. Rest assured!"

So wholly unexpected was this bold speech that no one thought of stopping it till the mischief was done. As a mighty cheer went up from the besieged, however, the infuriated soldiers of the investing army seized Katsutaka and in mad fury kicked and cuffed him mercilessly. Then at Katsuyori's command they crucified him just opposite the main gate of the castle he had given his life to save.

Early the next morning the allied forces came and the Kai army being utterly routed, the siege was raised.

THE WRESTLING OF A DAIMIO

The Wrestling of a Daimio

IN the second month of the fifteenth year of Tenshō (A.D. 1587), Toyotomi Hideyoshi, who had brought the greater part of Japan under his sway, crossed over to the Island of Kyūshū with a large army, in order to subjugate Shimazu Yoshihisa, an independent daimio governing eight of the nine provinces that form the island. The following month Gamō Ujisato, a renowned general in Hideyoshi's army, advanced to the Castle of Ganshaku in the province of Buzen, and attacked it fiercely for three successive days. The garrison, however, offered such a stubborn resistance that little impression was made; and it seemed unlikely that the fortress would fall into the hands of the besiegers for some time. Ujisato, being a man of impetuous and fiery disposition, lost all patience, and berated his men soundly.

"Cowards!" he shouted. "How is it you are so long in taking such an insignificant place? Have you all turned women? I will take the castle single-handed!"

He dashed to the front, spurring his steed recklessly forward in the very teeth of a volley of arrows and bullets that was directed at him. But as he neared the ramparts a shot struck his horse in the abdomen causing it, with a scream of agony, to rear itself up on its hind legs and throw its rider backwards off the saddle. At the instant, the gate of the castle was flung open, and a number of men rushed out. The fallen warrior encompassed by the foe thought his end had come, when a giant clad in black armour and mounted on a great chestnut horse dashed to the rescue. With mighty strokes he cut and hewed right and left, scattering the enemy like leaves before the wind of autumn. Some fell dead beneath the hoofs of his horse, others took to their heels and regained the shelter of the walls. Nishimura Gonshirō did not trouble himself to follow the fugitives, but leaping from his charger hastened to raise his chief. Ujisato was but slightly wounded, and with Gonshirō's help was able to mount the latter's horse.

"A thousand thanks, my gallant fellow," he said, gathering up the reins. "But for you I should by this time have been a dead man. I shall never forget you have saved my life this day, and it will be my great pleasure after the war to express my gratitude in some tangible form."

The example of Gonshirō's heroic deed seemed to put new spirit into Ujisato's men, and with greater determination and bravery they stormed the castle. As a result in the course of a few hours the garrison was obliged to surrender, and before many days had elapsed all Kyūshū had submitted to Hideyoshi's rule.

When quiet was restored Hideyoshi bestowed rewards on all the daimios who had fought for him, and Ujisato was promoted to the Governorship of Matsuzaka Castle in the province of Isé with an annual income of 300,000 *koku* of rice.

All in their turns, and according to their degrees, Ujisato rewarded those of his vassals who had distinguished themselves under his leadership. Some were given handsome gifts; others had their stipends raised. Gonshirō who considered he had done a greater deed than any of the others, seeing that he had saved his master's life at the risk of his own, naturally expected to receive some special favour. But greatly to his surprise and chagrin no acknowledgment was made. What could be the reason?

At first he felt no little resentment and brooded over this neglect. But after a time, being a man who cared little for gain, he let the affair fade from his mind though he still felt sore when he happened to think of it.

Meanwhile the summer had come and gone, and now the 15th of September was here. The night of all the year on which the atmosphere in Japan is most translucent and the moon shines with the greatest brilliancy. The night when men of a poetic turn sit up into the small hours composing verses on the beauty of the scene, the while they sip *saké* from delicate porcelain cups to aid the fickle muse. On this night therefore Ujisato gave a "moon-viewing party," inviting a large number of his retainers to a banquet in the main hall of his castle.

The witching light of the full moon wrapt the stern old pile; the tiny ripples on the moat glistened like liquid gold; the crickets shrilled musically among the tall grasses. The sliding screens had been removed and the calm beauty without softened and impressed the hearts of the sturdy warriors inured to scenes so different of bloodshed and the din of battle. Now it was that charmed by the loveliness around them many began to compose verses in adoration of the scene, and Ujisato's were among the best. But after a time the *saké* of which they partook, not sparingly, went to their heads, and it is not surprising that some of the would-be poets became a little elevated. The talk turned to tales of war and one and another recounted deeds of prowess performed by himself in the face of danger and difficulty. Nor was the host, Lord Ujisato himself, above a little boasting in his cups and it was thus he spoke:—

"Listen, my friends," he began. "Do you remember the fierce assault of the Castle of Ganshaku at the beginning of this year? The mere mention of it makes my blood boil! We attacked the castle three days without a break yet could make no headway. You men lost heart. To rouse you to a final effort I rode up to the gate alone—alone, in the face of the enemy amid a perfect hailstorm of missiles. A bullet struck my horse and he fell—I under him. Seizing the opportunity the enemy poured out and surrounded me nine or ten deep—I determined to sell my life dear" . . . here the narrator paused to wipe his face from which the perspiration was streaming from the energy with which he spoke. Gonshirō's heart leapt, he bent forward his face eager— now, at last his lord was about to reward his patient waiting and acknowledge his service before all men.

"To sell my life dear," repeated Ujisato with gleaming eyes. "So I fought as I had never done before with the courage of despair. Some I cut down, others I put to flight, finally I succeeded in remounting my horse and rode into the castle before the enemy could close the gates against me. Seeing my intrepid action you were inspired by my spirit, and following closely on my heels, you all did your best and the fortress was taken."

Thus did Ujisato omit all mention of Gonshirō and overlook his gallant deed. This base ingratitude was more than the faithful retainer could bear!

"Gonshirō begs permission to speak a word, your lordship," he said brusquely.

"By all means," assented Ujisato. "What is it?"

"Forgive me, your lordship, but what you said just now is hardly correct."

"What! You imply I spoke an untruth!"

"Yes, your lordship. You talk as if you had ridden into the castle unaided. That is not true. When you fell from your horse and were surrounded by the enemy's men I hastened to your rescue and it was my horse on which I assisted you to mount. By my timely help you were enabled to ride into the castle. It is but bare justice that you should amend your statement and acknowledge that you were saved from certain death by Gonshirō, your lordship."

This bold speech caused no little stir amongst the guests. Many of those present could bear witness to the truth of the rough soldier's words. They waited with bated breath for what would follow.

Ujisato was moved to make a frank avowal. It had long been in his mind to requite Gonshirō's great service by a suitable reward, and it was his intention to appoint him governor of the castle of Tagé which was a small fortress attached to the large castle of Matsuzaka where he himself resided. But Tagé Castle occupied a naturally strong site and stood in relation to the greater castle in such a situation that if a rebellion broke out in it, or if it were taken by an enemy, the safety of Matsuzaka would be immediately threatened. It was of the first importance, therefore, that it should be placed in the hands of an absolutely trustworthy man, and the cautious Ujisato wished to be quite sure of the loyalty of Gonshirō and to test him to the utmost before putting him in a position of so much importance and responsibility.

"Silence, Gonshirō!" thundered the daimio, keeping up the part he had decided to play a little longer. "How dare you say such a thing of your lord! Liar! I have no recollection of being saved by you or by any one else."

"Strange, my lord! Your words at the time were, 'A thousand thanks, Gonshirō! But for you I should have been dead by now. I shall never forget what you have done and after the war I will give you a reward.' I want no reward—I am a plain soldier with neither wife nor child—but it is unbearable that you should thus ignore my service. It is an undoubted fact, my lord, that I did save your life and thus opened the way for our troops to take the castle of Ganshaku."

"It is a lie! You did not save my life."

"It is the truth! I did save you!"

"You are drunk; you do not know what you are saying. I repeat, you did not save my life!"

Gonshirō's blood was up. He threw discretion to the winds.

"Ingrate and liar! I did save your life!"

"A lie!"

Ujisato frowned darkly and seemed about to have the daring offender punished as he deserved, but apparently changing his mind, he laughed good-humouredly and,

"Look here, Gonshirō," he said, "you insist that you saved me; I deny it. At this rate there can be no end of the matter for each holds to his own opinion. But to settle the question once for all let us have a wrestling bout, you and I. If I am beaten I will admit that you saved me as you aver, and prostrating myself before you with both hands on the ground I will humbly beg your pardon for what I have said. That will be as great an humiliation as removing one's helmet on the field of battle and surrendering to the foe. On the other hand, should you be thrown you will be branded as a liar and ordered to commit *seppuku*. Will you wrestle with me on those conditions?"

The guests were amazed. One whispered to another.

"What a proposal!"

"Monstrously unfair!"

"One contestant risks his life, the other a mere apology!"

"What are the chances?"

"Gonshirō is the better man."

"There I disagree with you—our lord has the greater skill. I wager his lordship will win."

"Gonshirō will never accept such conditions—they are too unequal!"

While these whispers were going round Gonshirō with head bent took an instant's thought. Then he looked up, stern defiance in his eye.

"My lord," he said, "I take up your challenge! I accept your conditions unfair though they be. I am a samurai and as such shrink from no danger. Strong in the truth of my cause I will wrestle with you."

"Good! At once. Prepare!"

"Your lordship, I am ready."

A space was cleared in the centre of the hall whilst the two champions divested themselves of all unnecessary clothing. Then the struggle began, and being well-nigh equally matched for some time neither gained any advantage over his opponent. At last, however, with a loud shout Gonshirō managed to twist his body, and by a dexterous movement raised his adversary on his shoulders, to throw him by a supreme effort down on to the mats at a distance of eight or nine feet. Ujisato swooned, and great was the consternation with which all rushed to his assistance. Restoratives were administered and to the relief of the company consciousness soon returned. The defeated combatant was able, leaning on the arm of an attendant, to retire to his own private apartments. The banquet, of course, was abandoned, most of the guests returning home. Gonshirō left the castle in great dejection and exasperation.

"What a fool my lord has shown himself," were his thoughts. "I could never have conceived it of him. I will remain in his service no longer. It is not on this place alone that the sun shines. A man of my prowess can find a billet anywhere. Heigh ho! I will go and seek service with some other daimio—some one I can respect more than I can my Lord Ujisato."

Having made up his mind it did not take Gonshirō long to get ready. At midnight he stole secretly away intending never to return.

The next morning all the samurai made their appearance at the castle to enquire after the health of their lord—all that is, but Gonshirō. The daimio who had quite recovered himself noticed his absence and calling Gamō Gonzaemon, one of his *karō*, or chief councillors, he asked what had become of him.

"I beg to inform, your lordship," replied the *karō*, "I have just heard a report that he has not been seen this morning and it is surmised that he has run away in consequence of the unfortunate occurrence of last evening."

"If that is true," exclaimed Ujisato, "I am indeed sorry. I did but dissimulate in order to test his fidelity, and if my words have lost me a good retainer I shall be much grieved. Order a search to be made and when he is found bring him instantly before me. Tell him I did but jest and that he shall have a liberal reward for the service he did me. Go at once, Gonzaemon; he cannot have gone far."

So the missing samurai was sought for in every likely and unlikely place, but without success. Nothing was seen or heard of him for many a long day.

An emaciated shabbily dressed *rōnin** carrying two swords with worn and ragged hilt-strings and rusty scabbards, and having on his dusty feet well-worn straw sandals, walked up, with the swagger peculiar to his caste, to the front door of Gonzaemon's residence.

"Insolent fellow!" cried the attendant whose business it was to answer the door. "This is not the place for you. If you would ask alms go to the back."

"I am no beggar to crave for alms," replied the stranger proudly. "I am one Nishimura Gonshirō, till three years ago in the service of Lord Ujisato. I have come to speak a word with your master. Kindly inform his honour of my visit."

Gonzaemon was delighted to hear of the return of the long vainly sought absenteé. To the disgust of the usher who looked with disdain on the dirty and travel-worn appearance of the

---

*A samurai who had renounced his clan and become a wanderer.

guest, he was admitted into the inner guest chamber. After a cordial greeting Gonzaemon asked:—

"And how have you been getting along since you left us so suddenly, Gonshirō?"

"But badly, your honour. They say 'a faithful servant never serves two masters,' but my case has been different. You see, I forsook my lord and of my own will became a *rōnin*. Hoping to enter the service of a more honourable chief I travelled from one province to another. But I was always unfortunate. Those whom I would have chosen to serve would have none of me—a deserter from another clan; those who would have accepted me were not good enough to suit my taste. After long and bitter experiences I have come to the conclusion that there is no daimio so worthy of allegiance as my former master, Lord Gamō. So I have come back to see if he will overlook my bad conduct in the past and let me re-enter his ranks. Of course, I do not expect to receive my former pay. I shall be grateful and more than satisfied if he will let me wait upon him as a humble attendant. Will you be so kind as to intercede for me?"

"You have done right to come back," answered the *karō*, kindly. "Sooth to say, our lord has greatly regretted his foolish jest and has caused strict search to be made to discover your whereabouts and if possible get you to return. He will rejoice to hear my news. Wait here and refresh yourself while I go and tell him."

Gonzaemon did not keep his visitor waiting long. He told Gonshirō that his lordship was pleased that he had come back and desired to see him at once.

"Excuse my mentioning such a thing," continued the *karō*, "but your garments are worn and travel-stained. May I not accommodate you with a change of apparel before you present yourself before his lordship?"

"On no account," returned the samurai. "You are very kind, but allow me to go as I am. My shabby condition will give my lord some idea of the hardships I have undergone as a *rōnin*."

"As you please, my independent fellow!"

The two men so different in aspect went up to the castle and waited in an ante-room till summoned to Lord Gamō's presence.

"Ah, Gonshirō!" he called out genially. "I am mightily glad to see you again. You were too hasty in running away. I was but teasing you and you took my words in bitter earnest. I hope you will take your old place and serve me as faithfully as before."

"Your kind words overwhelm me, your lordship," said Gonshirō humbly. "I have no words in which to express my sense of your clemency. I will henceforth serve you to the uttermost of my ability."

The good-natured Gonzaemon was delighted to witness this reconciliation between chief and vassal. The daimio ordered a feast to be prepared in honour of the occasion, and presently, over the good cheer, they all became very merry. It was not long before Ujisato began, as on a former occasion, to talk rather boastfully of his exploits and his prowess on the field.

"Gonshirō, when I wrestled with you that time, we all remember, I was beaten because I was half intoxicated," he said. "Since then my health has much improved and I am much heavier and stronger than before. On the other hand, your many hardships have greatly reduced you and you are a mere shadow of your former self. Should we try a bout now, you would have no chance at all."

It might have been thought that learning wisdom from bitter experience Gonshirō would have had the sense to agree with his lord's words, and to have said "That is very true, your lordship. It was but by a fluke that I won before; I should have not the slightest chance now." But foolish fellow that he was, he forgot everything but the supposed aspersion on his strength and skill which he could not allow to pass unchallenged.

"I am very thin as your lordship truly observes," he said bluntly, "but my strength is unabated. It is fitting that a samurai should be stronger than his chief. My muscles were hardened in many a field of battle and in friendly contests—they are like wires. Excuse me, but I could not be thrown though five—nay ten—men of your weight should set upon me at the same time."

"What, braggart! You still boast of your strength! Well, if you are so sure of yourself you shall wrestle with me again."

"With pleasure, your lordship!" said the undaunted samurai.

"Get ready!"

"I am ready, your lordship."

With these words the two men rose and prepared for the
struggle. Gonzaemon wondered at their infatuation. For years
Ujisato had regretted the act that had cost him a faithful
retainer. For years Gonshirō had wandered a *rōnin*, homeless,
and often without food. Chief and vassal had become reconciled
and all was going well, when, for the sake of a little paltry pride,
this happy state of things was again endangered and a perma-
nent estrangement might be the result. He strove to remon-
strate but neither would listen. All he could do was to advise
Gonshirō, by dumb signs, to allow himself to be beaten; and
Gonshirō coming too late to a better understanding of his rash
conduct answered in the same manner, "I will."

Satisfied that he had averted a catastrophe, the *karō* offered to
act as umpire, standing up with an open fan in his hand. After the
preliminary moves the combatants grappled, and a hard tussle it
was. Gonshirō honestly intended to let his master have the satisfaction of winning. "But," thought he, "if I let myself be thrown
too easily my lord will suspect something; besides I cannot let
him think me quite such a weakling as he would make out."
Warming to the fight he again thought, "If I allow myself to be
beaten, having strength to win, I should be a contemptible creature selling himself for the sake of his place and pay. Nothing dis-
graces a samurai so much as to be a flatterer. 'A man lives for but
one generation, but a good name lives forever.' A good name is
above all material rewards. I cannot pretend defeat. I must do
my best at all costs and come what may, throw my lord again."

Hereupon he braced his feet and bent his body, and with a
loud shout shouldered his opponent, and threw him down three
mats off just as he had done before.

The umpire never doubting that Gonshirō had followed his
counsel and that it was he who was thrown, ran forward,
exclaiming:—

"Well done, my lord! I never saw a better throw!"

He had no time to say more before he found out his mistake.
What was his dismay to find that Gonshirō was again the victor and
that it was his lord who had thus a second time suffered a humiliating defeat. It was too exasperating! The same story over again.

Now that his excitement had cooled down somewhat,

Gonshirō was covered with shame and mortification at what he had done.

Ujisato rose without assistance and stamping his foot as though in rage stalked off to an inner apartment.

"Fool that I am, I have done it again!" cried Gonshirō in despair. "In spite of your advice, in spite of my own determination, my vanity got the upper hand and forgetting all else I committed this unpardonable offence a second time. I will disembowel myself and I beg you to do me the honour to witness the act!"

So saying the unhappy man took up the short sword he had laid aside and was on the point of plunging it into his body, when the sliding door was hastily pushed open and Ujisato ran forward just in time to arrest his arm.

"Hold, hold! Gonshirō," he cried. "You are always too impetuous. I do not blame you for this—it is the true samurai spirit—the same spirit that in spite of want, of hunger and rags, disdains to flatter for the sake of gain. My brave fellow, I honour you for this! It might have been that the hardships of the last three years had changed your character—that you might now have been willing to sell your honour for my favour and worldly prosperity—so I feigned drunkenness and a boastful spirit that once more I might challenge you to fight and thus test you to the full. You have stood the test nobly. You disdained to flatter even at such a cost. You are indeed the pattern of all that a samurai should be! In recognition of your signal service to me at the storming of the Castle of Ganshaku I appoint you Governor of the Castle of Tagé with a stipend of 10,000 *koku*. As a reward for throwing me to-day in the face of every temptation to do otherwise I give you a further stipend of 1,000 *koku*; and in acknowledgment of the defeat I sustained at your hands three years ago you shall have another 1,000. Here is your writ of appointment."

At this unexpected magnimimity on the part of his lord even Gonshirō, hardened warrior though he was, could not restrain his tears.

In the years following, Gonshirō served his chief, Lord Gamō, faithfully and with devotion. When Ujisato was poisoned through the wiles of an adversary his loyal vassal killed himself in order to accompany his dearly loved master to Hades.

THE STORY OF
KIMURA SHIGENARI

The Story of
Kimura Shigenari

I

IN the eighteenth year of Keichō (A.D. 1613) Toyotomi Hideyoshi had been dead fourteen years and his son, Hideyori, now two and twenty should have been ruling over Japan as Regent in his stead. But his adherents had sustained a crushing defeat at the hands of the troops of his rival, Tokugawa Iyeyasu, at the battle of Sekigahara, and the tide of fortune had turned from him. All the daimios had given in their allegiance to Iyeyasu, and he was appointed Shogun by the Emperor. A few years later he abdicated in favour of his son Hidetada, though in reality he still steered the ship of state. On the other hand Hideyori's star had been fast declining. He was now merely the Lord of Settsu and Kawachi, comparatively small provinces, with the honorary title of "Minister of the Right." Nevertheless, in his stronghold, the "impregnable" Castle of Osaka, built by his father, Hideyoshi, at an enormous cost, there were still, it is said, some 100,000 men, among whom were many brave and loyal officers such as Katagiri Katsumoto, Sanada Yukimura, Susukida Hayato and Kimura Shigenari, the last of whom is the hero of this story.

A few powerful daimios, remembering with gratitude the great favours they had received from Hideyoshi, in secret still adhered to the cause of his son and watched for an opportunity to strike for the restoration of the Toyotomis' power and prestige. Iyeyasu, with his accustomed keen insight, perceived the situation and determined by one stroke to settle matters once for all. This was the state of affairs between the two great families, and it was felt that hostilities might break out again at any moment.

Shigenari now twenty years of age had served Hideyori as page and attendant since his childhood. His intelligence and loyalty, above all, his prowess in arms and knowledge of tactics had just led Hideyori's Prime Councillor, Katagiri Katsumoto, to promote him over the heads of some older men to a high rank in the army, with the title of Nagato-no-Kami, or Lord of Nagato province, and an annual allowance of 7,000 *koku* of rice. Mano Yorikané, one of Hideyori's veteran generals, admiring his courage and sterling character, gave tangible proof of his admiration by bestowing his beautiful and accomplished daughter, Aoyagi, on him for a wife.

With all his manly attributes and physical strength, Shigenari was exceptionally handsome, of a slender build, and possessed of a gentle graceful manner. At first glance it was his beauty and refinement that struck the beholder, not his strength and ability. For this reason those of the warriors who had not had opportunity to witness his skill as a soldier were inclined to regard his sudden promotion with wonder and some suspicion, one or two even going so far as to say—behind his back—"Shigenari is esteemed above his merits. He is effeminate and gentle; in war he will show cowardice and fly from the sounds of strife." Among the backbiters was a *chabōzu* or "tea-priest"* called Yamazoé Ryōkwan, a notorious bully and drunkard. Possessing undoubted skill in military arts and great muscular strength, he was apt to be boastful; and the idea seized him to pick a quarrel with Shigenari and thereby to provoke a contest between them and humiliate the courtly hero.

---

*A samurai of lower rank whose business it was to serve his lord with tea, and who was often master of the tea ceremonies. He had his head shaven like a priest—hence the name "tea-priest."

With this object Ryōkwan one day hid himself behind a screen; and as Shigenari passed hurriedly along the matted corridor on his way to the audience chamber, the tea-priest suddenly thrust his sheathed sword in his way. The surprised warrior leapt lightly over it, but the skirt of his *hakama* touched it as he did so. Ryōkwan sprang out of ambush.

"Kimura Dono, you go too fast!" he shouted angrily. Shigenari turned back.

"Excuse my rudeness," he said courteously.

"Your apology is too late! It came only after my demand."

"Forgive my double rudeness, Yamazoé, I was in such haste that I did not consider. Excuse me!"

"You speak like a fool! If you are late it is your own fault, and do you think you may tread on my sword with impunity? It is true that I am a tea-priest and your inferior in rank, yet I also am a samurai! A samurai's sword is his soul. You have trodden on my soul, and such an insult is inexcusable! Out of malice you did it. I challenge you to a duel!"

"You speak wildly; why should I bear malice towards you, or wish to insult you?"

"Then why did you tread on my sword?"

"I have already explained;—because I am in haste to present myself to my lord."

"Then allow me to do to you what I choose and I will accept your apology."

"By all means; do to me as you wish."

"I will take that!" and he struck a blow at Shigenari's cheek with all the force of his bare hand.

Shigenari smiled.

"Thank you for your chastisement!" he said, and went on his way.

Ryōkwan now strutted arrogantly about the castle, giving every one he met a highly-coloured account of what had occurred, and calling Shigenari "a white-livered samurai." Those who were jealous of Shigenari's promotion repeated the story in still more exaggerated terms, in consequence of which many samurai who had no real knowledge of the young officer's character believed the tale and laughed to scorn his supposed pusillanimity. Shigenari knew all about this, but did not let it disturb him at all.

Not so his father-in-law, Yorikané. Being fiery-tempered and extremely punctilious concerning points of honour, he no sooner heard of the incident than he hurried to Shigenari's residence and demanded to see him.

"Welcome, father-in-law," said the young man composedly. "Pray sit down."

"Sit down? No, I cannot sit down, and never again call me 'father.' I have come to tell you that you must divorce my daughter at once."

"This is very sudden! What reason can you give for your strange request?"

"Fool that I was to give my daughter to a white-livered samurai such as you!"

"Ha! Do you use such a term of me!"

"You feign ignorance! Well, then, I will tell you why men call you a coward. Listen! It is said you let your cheek be struck by that low tea-priest a day or two ago and he still lives to tell the tale! Has it passed from your mind so soon? Ah, I see you recollect it!"

"Surely, I remember that Ryōkwan struck my cheek with his hand, but what of it!"

"What of it? What of it? Can a samurai receive a deadly insult like that and suffer it to pass unnoticed! Coward! How came you to permit him to do it in the first instance?"

"Ryōkwan put his sword in my way as I was hurrying to the presence of my lord; the hem of my *hakama* just touched it as I passed over but the man insisted that I had trodden on it and by design. It is evident he meant to pick a quarrel with me in any case. I apologised, but he refused to listen. Deeming it waste of time to argue with a bully, to end the matter as speedily as possible, I let him strike me as he wished. That is the whole affair."

"Indolent coward!" exclaimed Yorikané, more incensed now that he heard Shigenari's account than he had been before. "Ryōkwan is a mere tea-priest, and you are a samurai of high rank in close attendance on our lord. There can be no comparison as to your respective standing—you should have killed him on the spot. Your conduct it totally inexplicable!"

"You are mistaken, father, when you say I should have killed him."

"How? There can be no two opinions on the matter. Where is your sense of honour? I will waste no more words on you. Let my daughter return home at once. I am ashamed to be called your father-in-law."

"Calm yourself, father, and hear me for but a moment. Do you imagine I overlooked Ryōkwan's insolent behaviour because I was afraid of him?"

"What else can I think?"

"Then listen. Recollect, father, that a samurai's life is not his own—it belongs to his liege lord. Judging from the strained relations between our clan and the Tokugawas hostilities may break out at any time . . ." here Shigenari's brow clouded and he sighed deeply; "Yes, war may break out at any moment now, and on the result hangs the future destiny of our lord and his clan. It is my intention to fight to the utmost of my strength and ability to requite if it be but the thousandth part of the many and great favours I have received from our gracious master. I shall sell my blood dear for his cause. And this is the bounden duty of every one of us, high and low alike. Our lives have never been more precious—not one can be spared except for the cause. If I had killed Ryōkwan out of resentment for a purely personal insult what good would it have done? Though his rank is inferior to mine, he is still a samurai; and as a samurai his death could not have been passed over unnoticed. Besides, Ryōkwan, though in human form, is but an insect in my estimation. It would be derogatory for a samurai to unsheathe his sword in anger against a mere insect! Therefore . . ."

"Enough, enough!" interposed the impulsive Yorikané. "I understand; you are right and I in my haste misjudged you entirely. Forgive me, and forget my thoughtless words."

Shigenari smiled, well pleased at the reconciliation.

"We are father and son again," went on the older man. "I am proud of the connection—you are a true samurai. But, tell me," he added with a chuckle. "You call Ryōkwan an insect; to what insect do you compare him?"

"To a fly," answered Shigenari. "A fly alights on filth or on an Emperor's crown—it makes no distinction between good and bad, high or low. But no one would call a fly an impolite insect. Looking on Ryōkwan as a man one feels anger and disgust; consider he is but a fly and it is unreasonable to have any such feelings, he is beneath them. Therefore I take no notice of anything he can do or say."

"Well argued, Shigenari! What a noble-minded man you are! I admire your wisdom and forbearance. As you say, the war cloud is fast darkening over us and it behoves all loyal samurai to be on their guard and not waste their energies on petty quarrels of their own. Again I ask your pardon for misconstruing your conduct. Though younger in years, dear Shigenari, you are older than I in judgment and forethought. Though old I am still as rash and impetuous as a boy."

More than satisfied with the explanation he had received, Yorikané returned home, and thenceforth did his best to clear his son-in-law from the imputation of cowardice. He spoke in glowing terms of Shigenari's real motive in his behaviour to the tea-priest, and told in what light he regarded him. Public opinion is ever quick to change; and those who had scoffed were soon loud in praise of Shigenari's self-repression and loyalty. Ryōkwan, on the other hand, was universally laughed at and nicknamed the "Fly-priest." As a natural consequence, instead of repenting of his misdeed, Ryōkwan's envy and hatred of his superior increased, and he was ever on the watch for a chance to vent his spite.

There was a large bath-room in the castle which was used in common by all. It was usual for the samurai on night duty to bathe several at the same time. One evening Ryōkwan happened to see Shigenari going into the bath-room, and thinking the time to satisfy his grudge had come, he followed him unobserved. The room was misty with the dense vapour rising from the hot water, and four or five samurai were already in the large square bath. Taking one of them to be Shigenari the tea-priest approached, and mustering all his strength, struck his head a heavy blow. The naked man sprang out of the water, and seizing Ryōkwan by the collar threw him on the floor where he returned the blow he had received with compound interest.

"I will teach you to strike a defenceless man without provocation!" he roared. "Do you know who I am? Susukida Hayato! Prepare for instant death!" Then seeing who it was he was belabouring, he exclaimed in astonishment:—

"Why, it's Ryōkwan, the contemptible Fly-priest! What is your object in striking my head as you did? You will find that though you are only a fly you cannot insult Susukida with impunity!"

Frightened almost out of his wits at the mention of the name Susukida, that of a hero renowned far and wide for his muscular strength, Ryōkwan stammered out:—

"I humbly beg your pardon, Susukida Sama; it was a mistake. I should never think of striking you, the blow was intended for Kimura Shigenari. Spare my life, I implore you!"

But this speech only incensed Susukida still further.

"What?" he cried. "Would you strike your benefactor?—the man who generously pardoned your outrageous conduct to him? Miscreant, I will deal a blow for my friend Kimura. Die!"

With these words Susukida raised his iron fist and assuredly Kyōkwan's last hour had come had it not been that some one caught the hand before it fell. Mad with rage Susukida struggled to free himself but in vain—he was held as in a vice. Twisting round he saw to his surprise that his captor was none other than Shigenari himself.

"Excuse my rudeness, Susukida Dono. Without doubt it is as the coward says—he mistook you for me, a circumstance for which I am extremely sorry. It is natural you should resent such an insult, but if you strike him with your fist you will kill him on the spot. He is my enemy; may I request you to leave his chastisement to me?"

"Of course," replied Susukida with a laugh and nod of assent as Shigenari released him. "It is for you to deal with him as you think best. I am told the fellow grows more arrogant and behaves with increasing rudeness to our comrades every day. I trust you will see that he has cause to repent."

As soon as Susukida had left the room, Shigenari helped

Ryōkwan to get up, and very kindly assisted him to his own chamber where he attended to his bruises with great solicitude. When the tea-priest had recovered somewhat, Shigenari said to him, gently remonstrant:—

"How foolish it is of you, Ryōkwan, to be so proud of your strength and in consequence to behave so arrogantly to your comrades and superiors. A samurai should use his gifts for his lord's service only. You should exert yourself solely for the benefit of His Highness Lord Hideyori. It is regrettable that you should waste your powers in causeless quarrels and fights. It was fortunate for you that it was I you insulted the other day; had it been some one else you would undoubtedly have paid for it with your life on the instant. You have superior muscular power and no little skill in the use of arms; now that war is so imminent the life of every samurai is precious; that is why I spared you—that you might live to serve in time of need. But you did not understand my motive and sought occasion to insult me again. How undiscriminating! If I had not interceded for you just now you would have died a useless death at the hands of Susukida Dono. Is not a purposeless death like that dishonour for a samurai? If you repent your past mistakes I will ask Susukida Dono to overlook and pardon your rudeness, and I am sure he will not refuse. Will you not amend your conduct and from henceforth direct all your energies to doing your very best for our lord and his cause, Ryōkwan?"

To this long speech delivered with a winning earnestness that pierced him to the heart, Ryōkwan listened with bent head and averted eyes. A few hot tears stole down his rough cheeks; he brushed them away with his sleeve before he answered in a broken voice.

"Every word you have uttered has cut me to the heart, Kimura Sama," he said. "Your kindness overwhelms me. I am deeply ashamed of myself, and I now see how blind I was not to perceive your noble and unselfish motives in the way you acted. Oh, that I might commit *seppuku* in atonement! But to take my life would be in opposition to your kind instruction: as you have pointed out it is the duty of us all to live till we die in our lord's cause. . . . If you can forgive me it is my earnest desire that you will take me for your own retainer. Unworthy though I am, I entreat you will not deny my request."

Touched and pleased at the success of his remonstrance, Shigenari gladly agreed to do as Ryōkwan asked. Having obtained permission from Lord Hideyori, they exchanged vows as master and retainer; and thus the brawling, overbearing drunkard of a tea-priest became a changed man, and with all the strength of a strong nature devoted himself to the service of the master he adored.

II.

The year following the events just narrated, the strained relations between the rivals, the Toyotomis and Tokugawas snapped, and as had been foreseen war was declared. The Ex-Shogun Iyeyasu and the reigning Shogun Hidetada with an army of 200,000 men lay siege to the Castle of Osaka, though as yet they did not venture on very close quarters. The besieged troops, though outnumbered by the enemy, were well commanded by numerous veteran generals and defended themselves with courage and skill. In several small engagements which took place without the castle, Iyeyasu's men, ensnared with artfully constructed stratagems, suffered severe defeat. Above all they sustained signal reverses at the hands of Shigenari who manœuvered adroitly and fought bravely with his company.

The siege lasted several months and still the brave little garrison held the enemy at bay. With each success their spirits rose. The shrewd Iyeyasu, seeing the impossibility of taking the stronghold by force and hopeless of starving it out, deemed it would be the best policy to patch up peace in some way, and trust to the pride and arrogance of the opposing faction to bring about their own downfall. Therefore, most cunningly, through the Emperor's mediation as it seemed, he proposed, nay, almost dictated peace to Hideyori. Most of his generals, including Sanada Yukimura, Chief of the General Staff, and Shigenari, considering the present situation favourable to the triumph of their side, emphatically opposed such a fatal act; but Hideyori's infamous and beautiful mother Madame Yodogimi who had great influence over her son, being persuaded to that effect by her licentious and thoughtless favourites who were weary of the confinement necessitated by the siege, threw all the weight of her maternal authority on the acceptance of the terms. Furthermore, the proposal coming from the highest quarter could hardly be slighted; therefore the defenders were almost without option compelled to agree to the humiliating terms proposed, which were that Hideyori should destroy the outer moat of his castle—to show the sincerity of his peaceful intentions— while Iyeyasu, in return, should cede to him the provinces of Kii and Yamato.

A day was appointed for the formal signing of the treaty; and Shigenari was nominated special envoy for the occasion, with Kōri Shumenosuké for vice-envoy.

Iyeyasu had the entrance to his camp strictly guarded; and with a view to displaying his authority before all the daimios assembled to witness the ceremony, he secretly instructed his most trusted generals to humiliate the expected envoys as much as possible. These officers who felt much chagrin at their frequent defeats were only too glad to have opportunity to wreak vengeance on the enemy by affronting their representatives.

Shigenari and Shumenosuké arrived on horseback, escorted by a little band of some eighty men. On their appearance before the camp of Tōdō Takatora, the sentinels one after the other called out:—

"Halt, sirs! As His Highness's camp is so near you must dismount."

Shumenosuké hurriedly pulled up and was about to get off his horse; but his superior stopped him with a gesture, and looked haughtily at the men in front. He cried loudly:—

"We are Kimura Shigenari and Kōri Shumenosuké, the representatives of Lord Toyotomi, Minister of the Right. No code of etiquette requires anyone to dismount before his equal in rank. You are insolent! We proceed."

Then Shigenari rode calmly forward followed by his suite.

When the envoys came to General Ii's camp his sentinels likewise demanded that they should dismount.

Giving the same reply as before, Shigenari, disregarding their attempts to stop him, put spurs to his horse and rode on.

At the camp of Lord Echigo more strenuous efforts were made to force the strangers to proceed on foot. In great wrath Shigenari protested against such unwarranted discourtesy.

"What mean you by such conduct?" he cried. "Judging from our reception I conclude it is the intention of Iyeyasu to disregard the Imperial mandate to make peace. Well, then, it is useless to go further. We will return at once to the castle and report to our lord the shameful treatment we have received!"

So saying he turned his horse and was about to go back, when Lord Echigo's men seeing they had gone too far, apologised profusely and begged him to pass on to fulfil his mission.

At length the envoys came to the entrance of the building where they were to meet the great Ex-Shogun. Here they dismounted and carrying their swords were about to enter when two ushers intercepted them, crying:—

"Your weapons must be left without!"

In no wise discomposed Shigenari said sternly:—

"It is a rule with a samurai never to leave his sword behind when he goes into an enemy's camp, on any pretext whatever."

This being an indisputable fact, the ushers could say no more, but led them armed as they were to the spacious apartment which had been prepared for the ceremony. A large number of daimios already occupied their places on two sides of the room. With a manner composed and dignified, Shigenari strode into the assembly in no whit daunted by the many hostile looks cast upon him, and took the seat to which he was directed in the centre, facing at a short distance the dais prepared for Iyeyasu when he should make his appearance.

Shumenosuké closely followed the deportment of his chief, and took his seat beside him.

Two Masters of the Ceremonies informed them that His Highness would be there presently. "And," they added, "as it is disrespectful to carry swords in his august presence you will kindly take them to the ante chamber and leave them there."

"Disrespectful!" thundered Shigenari in tones that reverberated through the hall. "To whom do you address such a word.

Recollect that we are the honourable representatives of the Minister of the Right! The disrespect is on your side and if you repeat your insolence you will have to answer for it!"

And he glared so fiercely on the two officials that they withdrew in consternation.

In a short time Iyeyasu, accompanied by many attendants, made his appearance and with impressive solemnity took his seat. All the daimios bowed reverently, and awed by his majestic demeanor and the example of others, Shumenosuké did the same. But Shigenari deigned to give the great statesman but the slightest acknowledgment and calmly looked him straight in the face.

"I am glad to see you, Shigenari," said Iyeyasu mildly. "Thank you for coming on this important mission. Your father Hitachi-no-suké and I were intimate friends and I am much indebted to him."

"Pardon me, your Highness," replied Shigenari, "but to-day I am the messenger of the Minister of the Right and private matters are out of place."

The tactful Iyeyasu, though put in the wrong, showed not the slightest trace of embarrassment. Producing a document from a receptacle in his hand, he passed it to Shigenari by an attendant and said quietly:—

"Kindly see that this is correct, Shigenari."

Shigenari carefully read over the paper which ran as follows:—

"In compliance with an Imperial Edict, Iyeyasu and Hideyori agree to make peace, on the sole condition that Hideyori fill up the outer moat of his castle as a token of his peaceful intentions. Either of the parties concerned who first appeals to arms henceforth, shall be guilty of disobeying the Imperial Mandate and shall be treated accordingly.

"Keicho 19, 12th month, 27th day."

As he read Shigenari's face grew darker and darker, and when he came to the end he started to his feet and exclaimed indignantly:—

"Are these your terms of peace, Your Highness? If so you have already disobeyed the Imperial command! Prepare!"

Sword in hand it seemed as if he were about to attack the old statesman. All present started up and sought to intercept the thrust. Iyeyasu, alarmed, raised both hands in deprecation and bade the young man resume his seat.

"Calm yourself, I pray you," he said hastily. "Old age makes me forgetful. By mistake I have shown you the wrong paper— here is the right one."

The crafty statesman produced another document from the case he held and handed it to Shigenari. It is hardly necessary to explain that this was an artifice. Iyeyasu had caused to be prepared two documents in different terms. Should the envoys accept the first in which all the advantage was on his side his intention was to keep back the other in which were stated the real conditions of the treaty. Shigenari had been too astute for him. He now examined the new document which read thus:—

"VOWS OF PEACE

"Article I.—In compliance with an Imperial Command, Iyeyasu and Hideyori vow to make peace and to enter into friendly relations.

"Article II.—Hideyori shall destroy the outer moat of his Castle, and Iyeyasu shall in return cede to him the provinces of Kii and Yamato by January next.

"Article III.—Immediately on the signing of the Vows of Peace, Iyeyasu shall disband his army and depart for Yamato.

"Article IV.—Either of the parties who violates the above vows and resorts to arms shall be found guilty of disobedience to the Imperial Command and shall be punished by the gods.

"Keichō 19, 12th month, 27th day."

Shigenari read the paper carefully several times.

"This is correct, Your Highness. Be pleased to put your signature and seal."

Iyeyasu complied. The envoy receiving it back put it into a bag made of rich brocade. Then bowing courteously, he said gravely though not without a touch of sarcasm:—

"I beg to congratulate Your Highness."

Then turning to the assembled daimios he bowed to them
also saying:—

"I thank you for your attendance."

Receiving their salutations in return, he once more made an
obeisance to Iyeyasu.

"Allow me to take my leave, Your Highness. Farewell, Your
Highness and your Excellencies."

With graceful courtesy he bowed once more and with his sub-
ordinate left the audience-chamber. All were constrained to
admire his noble bearing and courage.

III.

Hideyori faithfully observed his part of the "Vows of Peace,"
and the outer moat which had constituted the greatest element
in the "impregnability" of his castle was filled up and levelled
with the ground. But Iyeyasu who had never had the least intention of fulfilling his part of the treaty held back the stipulated
provinces in spite of all the demands of Hideyori. Hence in the
spring of the following year hostilities were resumed, and a
great army commanded by Iyeyasu once more invested the
Castle of Osaka.

The garrison made a stubborn resistance for some weeks; but
the fortress was now shorn of its main protection, and most unfortunately the discord between Madame Yodogimi's favourite generals and the other officers assumed formidable dimensions. In
consequence, the defenders were severely defeated in more than
one engagement, and their numbers were so greatly reduced that
it was impossible for them to hold the castle much longer.

One night Sanada Yukimura, the Chief of the General Staff,
met Shigenari in secret.

"It is not possible for us to hold out," he said gloomily. "We
must effect the escape of our lord out of the castle and convey
him to a place of security—he can take refuge in the province of
Lord Shimazu. Through him we may be able to do something to
retrieve our losses and restore the power of our clan. Some of us
must go with our chief, but in order the more easily to get away
the enemy must be deluded with the idea that Hideyori and his

bravest warriors have fallen; therefore we must leave substitutes behind us who resemble us in some degree. Their bodies will be found, and the enemy will think we are dead and not try to pursue us as they most certainly would do if they thought we had fled. I have found my substitute; do you find yours. I must regret that it is necessary for these men to sacrifice their lives for ours, but we must all act for the future good of the clan to which we owe allegiance—all personal considerations must give way. Do you not approve of my plan?"

"It is an excellent idea," replied Shigenari, after some reflection. "And I heartily approve of it. But if every experienced general leaves the castle even though substitutes are left, the shrewd Iyeyasu will soon suspect the truth. I at any rate must remain. I was seen by Iyeyasu and his staff only a short time ago; they will not have forgotten my features and cannot be deceived by another man clad in my armour. Therefore, I leave the escort of our lord and the restoration of the clan to you and the other generals. I will stay alone with the garrison and fight to the last. My death and your life are equally necessary for the sake of our lord. So do not seek to dissuade me. I am resolved."

"A truly noble resolve, my friend," said Yukimura with admiration. "Would that I could remain with you! I am reluctant to leave you alone and we shall miss your help, but if you are determined to do this thing far be it from me to dissuade you. It must be well-known to the enemy that you are a favourite of our lord and always in close attendance on his person; so when they find your dead body on the field they will never suspect he has escaped. Your death in this way will be the means of restoring the power of the Toyotomis. I could find it in my heart to envy you, good comrade!"

"Then that is settled. To-morrow I will charge the enemy's line with my men and divert his attention while the rest of you steal out from the rear."

After a few words of affectionate farewell, the two men parted knowing they would never meet again.

On retiring to his room for a brief rest, Shigenari spoke to his young wife in his usual cheerful manner.

"To-morrow our troops are going to make a sally that will

effectually dispose of the enemy," he said. "On such a notable occasion I wish to wear the armour my lord graciously gave me last year; pray bring it to me."

When his wife brought it he took the helmet; and burning some very precious incense called *Ranjatai*, held the helmet so that the smoke ascended into it. Aoyagi, divining from his manner that he had some solemn motive for this action, felt her heart sink.

"You intend to die fighting in to-morrow's engagement:—is it not so, my husband?"

"Die fighting?" said Shigenari. "Why do you ask? Does not a soldier always take his life in his hand when he goes to the field of battle?"

"Yes, but there is some special reason why I think you will fall to-morrow. I have often heard that a warrior burns incense into his helmet when he is determined to die on the field. I know the castle will fall before long and I am sure you mean to give up your life in to-morrow's battle. Do not seek to deceive me. I am the daughter of a samurai. I will not let you die alone."

"My brave wife! Forgive my hesitation in disclosing to you my resolve. I forebore to take you into my confidence fearing just this thing."

He then gave his wife an account of his conversation with Sanada Yukimura and of their decision.

"Though I give up my life for my lord," he concluded, "do not be so rash as to die with me. It is my wish that you should live and pray for the prosperity of our lord. Live for his sake. It is my last request."

"Your wish is my law," answered his wife. "I will obey you. I know you will die a glorious death and leave undying fame behind you!"

Then Aoyagi brought *saké* and two tiny cups in which they drank to their long farewell. That ceremony over, Aoyagi excused herself and retired to her own apartment. As she did not return, Shigenari, wondering at her long absence, went to seek her; and to his horror and amazement found that she had committed suicide with a short sword that lay beside the lifeless body. A written paper explained her rash act.

"Husband," it ran, "forgive my dying before you. I meant to obey you, but I cannot do so. Kō-u of China, though a brave warrior overcome with grief at parting with his wife, hesitated shamefully before going to his last battle. In our country Kiso Yoshinaka showed the same weakness. Not for a moment do I compare you to those men, but still I think that I, who losing you shall have no further hope in this world, had better die now before you fight your last fight and go to wait for you in Hades. Do your best against the foe! We shall meet again in the Spirit World—till then farewell! Aoyagi."

The morning of the next day broke clear and cloudless. It was the first day of the fifth month in the twentieth year of Keichō (1615).

A large force under the command of Ii Naotaka advanced from the enemy's camp and rushed to the attack. Shigenari met them at the head of seven hundred cavalry, and a fierce struggle took place. With the strength of desperation Shigenari's company, though so inferior in numbers, beat back the foe. But as one regiment was beaten, another and yet another dashed forward to take its place, and it was impossible that the castle party could win in the end.

"We must cut our way into the main regiment," said Shigenari during a short breathing space to his faithful retainer Ryōkwan— once known as the "Tea-priest"—"If we can only manage to kill Ii Naotaka, the Commander in Chief, the enemy will be disheartened and we may have some chance."

Then inspired by the example of their leader, the little band hurled themselves on the foe: and unable to stand against such fury, the fourth and fifth companies fell back in disorder, and it seemed that a general rout would be the result.

Ii alone stood his ground. Brandishing his *saihai* or baton he roared in stentorian tones:—

"Cowards! Do you fly before such a handful of men? Back, back, and the day is ours!"

His words took instant effect. His flying troops rallied, maintained their position and fought bravely. Seeing this, Shigenari smiled grimly to himself.

"Now is my time to break through the lines, kill Ii and then die!"

Putting spurs to his horse he darted forward swift as a flash of lightning, his brilliant helmet and shining armour gleaming in the sun. Ryōkwan followed close with his heavy iron rod, and the rest of the devoted band strove to keep up, cutting and hewing their way through the ranks. So violent was their onset that again Ii's men wavered. At this critical juncture Seki Jūrozaemon, a samurai noted for his huge strength, suddenly appeared and struck at Shigenari with a great halbert; but Shigenari's spear point pierced clean through his breastplate of mail and he fell dead from his horse. Ii's soldiers were panic-stricken and none ventured to oppose Shigenari who continued his onward rush and attacked Ii before he had time to escape. Being no match for his assailant, Ii must have fallen had it not been for one Fujita Noto-no-Kami who came to his rescue. Furious at this check Shigenari turned to throw him from the saddle with a single thrust, and in that moment Ii managed to escape.

Looking back, Shigenari could see but few of his men; nearly all had fallen in the mêlée. Severely wounded, and faint with loss of blood, Shigenari realised that he could do no more. Unnoticed he alighted from his spent horse and retired to a small grove on some elevated ground. His approach was observed by a low fellow belonging to Ii's camp who was hiding behind the trees. Such was the estimation in which Shigenari was held that even in his weakness he inspired awe and dread. The skulking coward did not dare to attack him openly, but as the wounded hero lay gasping on the ground stole softly up behind him and aimed a blow to his head. Shigenari heard the slight rustle of his approach and turned, whereupon the wretch made off. Shigenari called him back.

"Fellow," he said, "whoever you are, come here and take my head."

But the man fearing some trick hesitated to obey.

"Coward," cried the dying warrior, "you have nothing to fear from me. Cut off my head, but I conjure you not to remove the helmet till you present it to your master, Iyeyasu. I am impatient—cut off my head as I bid you."

As he spoke Shigenari lifted the lower plates of his helmet and stretched out his neck for the blow. As in a trance the craven crept up and severed the head from the body. Then gaining courage he raised the dripping trophy high in the air and shouted at the top of his voice:—

"I, Andō Chōzaburō, single-handed, have taken the head of Nagato-no-Kami Shigenari, the most renowned warrior in the Osaka Army!"

The boast reached the ears of a man covered with blood who was still in the thick of the fray. It was Ryōkwan.

"My Lord, Nagato-no-Kami, was not the man to be killed by such a weakling as Andō," he cried, as loudly as his failing strength would permit. "He had some reason for allowing his head to be cut off. Remember that, my enemies."

With that he stabbed himself in his abdomen and expired.

After the battle the head of Shigenari, enclosed in its helmet, was taken to Iyeyasu for inspection. It had been the desire of all that day to get the head of the hero, and Iyeyasu had the helmet removed for verification. As this was done the sweet odour of incense floated through the air.

The old statesman surveyed the noble features with something of reverent admiration.

"Never was a more loyal or courageous samurai than Nagato-no-Kami!" he said slowly. "Would that I had many like him!"

The attempted escape from the castle proved a failure. On May 8th, the besiegers once more attacked the castle on all sides, and there ensued one of the bloodiest struggles in the history of Japan. It resulted in the complete overthrow of Hideyori's faction and the destruction of the castle by fire. The unfortunate nobleman, his mother and all the maids of honour perished in the flames.

HONEST KYŪSUKÉ

Honest Kyūsuké

GONZAEMON, the head-man of the village of Tamamura in the province of Kōdzuké, whose family had from generation to generation enjoyed a large fortune, employed a number of servants. Among them was one named Kyūsuké who had been added to the household on the recommendation of a peasant of the same village as being exceedingly honest. Though he was very young, unlike other servants, he worked very hard and performed all his duties as well when no one observed him as under the eye of his master. Gonzaemon, therefore, began to look upon him as a great acquisition and took a keen interest in him.

One day he summoned Kyūsuké to his room and said:—

"Kyūsuké, I am pleased to see that you always work faithfully, but I think I should be more pleased if you would leave off working at an earlier hour in the evening and go to bed at the same time as your fellow-servants. If you continue to be so much more industrious than they there will be complaints among them."

"My good master," answered the young man, "though I do not like to disobey you, I regret to say that I can never get to sleep before nine o'clock at night."

"You surprise me," said Gonzaemon, "but at least you can oblige me by remaining in bed until the usual hour for getting up in the morning."

"My good master," replied Kyūsuké again, "I am very sorry to displease you so often, but mine is a hopeless case, for to be frank with you I cannot for the life of me stay abed after seven in the morning."

Now, you must know, that according to our old way of counting time, nine at night was midnight, and seven in the morning answered to 4 o'clock. Kyūsuké, therefore, never slept more than four hours every night, and his master on learning this was surprised beyond measure.

"What a wonder you are!" he explained. "It is seldom one finds gentlemen in service such passionate lovers of work! How gratified I am to find such a notable exception in you. I trust you will not take my suggestion amiss; it was necessary in order that your fellow-servants should not suffer in consequence of your zeal for work."

"I humbly beg your forgiveness for venturing to disobey your kind orders," said the young man respectfully.

"Don't beg my forgiveness," said his master, "for by so doing you put me in an awkward position."

After considering for a few moments while the servant waited silently for further orders, Gonzaemon resumed:—

"Well, Kyūsuké, I have another suggestion to offer you. You know that you are your own master while your fellow-servants are asleep. I do not wish you to work for me in those hours, so if you do not wish to rest, employ that time in making sandals for your own profit. I will see that you are provided with plenty of straw."

"My good master, you are very kind, but I fear it is not right that a servant should use any of his time in work for his own profit."

Thus Kyūsuké once more baffled the kind intentions of his master. Gonzaemon was struck with his faithfulness.

"If you persist in refusing all my proposals I shall be at a loss what to do with you," he said. "So be pleased to do as I request you only this once."

Kyūsuké could not refuse his master's kindness so delicately offered, and he consented to use his spare time for his own profit. Henceforth the early morning and late evening hours were devoted to the task of making *waraji* or straw sandals, which he sold to a kitchen-ware dealer in the village, thereby making a small but regular income, every *sen* of which he intrusted to his kind master for safe keeping. Soon the young servant's diligence became known, and the country people encouraged his industry by always asking for the "Kyūsuké *waraji*" in preference to any other. This naturally pleased the dealer who continually pressed Kyūsuké for further supplies. Gonzaemon, likewise pleased at the success of his plan, determined to lend out the money in his charge so as to increase the amount by good interest. In this he found no difficulty for people had the idea that some luck attached itself to anything connected with the honest servant, and were only too glad to be accommodated with loans out of his savings.

Thus eight years passed away and Kyūsuké was still a servant in the household of Gonzaemon. One day the latter called the young man into his apartment and addressed him as follows:—

"My dear Kyūsuké, time indeed flies like an arrow, as the proverb says. Eight years have elapsed since I was so fortunate as to take you into my service. You have never squandered your wages as other servants do; setting apart a certain amount for small personal expenses you have regularly committed to my care all that you earned. I should certainly have proved but a poor banker, had I not sought some profitable investment for your deposits. All these years I have been lending out your money at a moderate rate, and it is astonishing to find how much your capital now amounts to. Behold! Your savings with interest and compound interest now reach the sum of one hundred *ryō!* Now, what do you propose to do with all this money?"

"My good master," said Kyūsuké, quite taken aback at the idea of such wealth, "you must be joking!"

"Not at all; it is as I say. Will you continue to lend it out, or would you prefer to dispose of it in some other way? It is for you to decide."

"A hundred *ryō!*" gasped Kyūsuké. "Did you really say 'one hundred *ryō*'?"

"A hundred *ryō!*" replied his master smiling.

"It is unbelievable!" said Kyūsuké.

"Your own industry is responsible for it," said Gonzaemon. "Now tell me what you are going to do with it."

Kyūsuké pondered long and deeply. At length he spoke.

"Kind master, if you would not think it taking an unpardonable liberty, I should much like to take the money and pay a short visit to my native place next spring."

"By all means," said Gonzaemon. "Do you know of a good investment in your native place?"

"No," answered Kyūsuké, readily enough now. "But you will understand better if I tell you a little of my family history. Excuse the liberty I take in troubling you with my affairs. I am the second son of a peasant, Kyūzaemon by name, living in the village of Shimo-Ogita-mura near Nanao, in the province of Noto. My elder brother, after leading a dissipated life and causing his parents much grief, suddenly left home and has never been heard of since. My mother died soon after, and my father married a widow with one daughter. Before long my stepmother took it into her head to adopt a son to marry her daughter and succeed my father as head of the family. Me she hated, and consequently treated me so unkindly, that I was soon convinced it would be for the happiness of all parties that I should leave home and go right away. So one day, leaving a letter of apology behind me, I secretly came away. At first I had rather a hard time of it, but since I was so lucky as to become your servant I have had nothing to complain of. I cannot sufficiently thank you for all your kindness to me." Here Kyūsuké paused, and bowed low, while tears filled his eyes. Conquering his emotion he resumed:—

"One hundred *ryō*, the largest sum of money I have ever set eyes on, I owe entirely to your goodness—how can I thank you? That I may make a proper use of your gift—for so I consider it—I shall return to my father and with this money buy him some ricefields. In addition, should my step-sister still remain single I shall try to find her a suitable husband. Having done this and established my family so that it will be in no danger of extinction, I shall make all haste to return to you and beg to offer you my lifelong service as some small way of requiting all you have done for me."

Gonzaemon was greatly touched.

"Kyūsuké," he said, "you are a noble fellow! A dutiful son as well as a faithful servant. I admire your laudable intention. 'To your old home return in splendour' says an old proverb, so Kyūsuké, return in splendour indeed! I will make it my business to provide the clothes you shall wear, and I will also see that you have suitable presents to take to all your relations."

Thus the conversation ended and Kyūsuké retired to pursue his usual avocations.

Early the following year, in spite of his servant's remonstrances, Gonzaemon, as good as his word, prepared all the necessary garments for Kyūsuké to wear in order to make a good impression on his visit home, and presents for each member of his family. Further, he pressed upon Kyūsuké's acceptance a short sword for protection on his journey, ten *ryō* for travelling expenses, and five *ryō* as a parting gift. Producing Kyūsuké's own hundred *ryō* he said:—

"Now, my dear Kyūsuké, you had better not carry this large sum in cash for fear you might get robbed on the way; I advise you to send it by bill of exchange."

"Indeed, no, good master," replied Kyūsuké. "That is quite unnecessary; who would suspect that a fellow of my sort had any money about him and attempt to rob me? It will be quite safe in the bosom of my dress."

"But you might lose it in some other way," persisted Gonzaemon. "You had better do as I say,—one cannot be too much on one's guard while travelling."

Kyūsuké laughed.

"Do not be uneasy on my account," he said. "I will be careful."

"As you please, Kyūsuké; but at least listen to me in one thing; while on your journey always make it a rule to start late in the morning, and to put up early in the evening. Above all never take a travelling companion, and do not speak of your affairs."

"I will bear in mind what you say, and most certainly follow your advice," said Kyūsuké. "A thousand thanks for all your favours, kind master. I can never forget all I owe to you."

With affectionate words on both sides Kyūsuké and his master parted and the young man set out on his journey homewards. But once upon the road the dutiful son, too eager to set his eyes once more on the village of his forefathers, was indiscreet enough to travel from the earliest hours of the day till late at night. So it was, that when he was in the neighbourhood of Oiwaké in the province of Shinano he one night lost his way in the darkness, and after a long march of five or six *ri* found himself in the middle of an extensive moor without a trace of human habitation.

"What shall I do?" he asked himself. "I fear I have been too rash. Had I followed my master's advice I should not be in this plight. It is only what I deserve."

Plodding on Kyūsuké was overjoyed after a time to observe a glimmer of light in the distance. Taking heart at this sign of a dwelling of some kind, he bent his weary steps toward it, and by and by came to a tumble-down cottage which appeared to be the only habitation for miles around. Kyūsuké went up to the door and called for admittance.

"Be good enough to show favour to a stranger! I am very sorry to disturb you at this late hour, but have lost my way and cannot find the road. Please let me in and tell me how to get to the nearest inn."

The door opened and a woman appeared. She was about thirty and poorly dressed and her coiffure was of a mean style, but there was something in her person that seemed to contradict the idea that her birth was as low as her surroundings.

"Come in," she said. "But you must not stay. I am indeed sorry for you, for you stand in the middle of one of Shinano's many moors. Whichever way you turn you must walk about five *ri* before you come to another house."

Kyūsuké being very tired requested the woman to give him a night's lodging, but she shook her head.

"Why did you come here?"

"I have told you; I lost my way and I saw a light. You cannot be so inhuman as to refuse me shelter for a few hours,—I ask no more."

"You will not want to stay when I tell you that this is the house of a robber—a highwayman."

"A robber!" Kyūsuké thinking of his treasure was alarmed. "Excuse me, I must go at once."

"Will you not rest a few moments?"

"By no means. How can I sit down in what I have learned is the residence of a highway-gentleman? Allow me to say Goodnight; I am much obliged to you."

Kyūsuké was for going at once but the woman stopped him.

"Good traveller, I must tell you that you are encompassed by danger in every direction. After all, I think the safest course for you to pursue is to remain here for the night and I will hide you from my husband. He will not be back for some time yet."

The manner and speech of the woman inspired confidence, so Kyūsuké deemed it prudent to abide by her advice. Taking off his large bamboo hat that he wore as a protection from both sun and rain, he sat down on the boarded floor of the kitchen glad to rest his weary limbs at last. The woman hurriedly prepared a simple supper for him, which he ate with relish, though in haste, as he feared the return of the master. The woman then led him to a wood-shed at the back of the cottage and said:—

"You would be in great danger should my husband discover you. So keep yourself hidden in this shed and do not mind a little discomfort. As soon as it is day and my husband goes out, I will let you out and you can continue your journey in safety."

Kyūsuké thanked her warmly, and had not long ensconced himself among the piles of firewood, making himself as comfortable as he could under the circumstances, when he heard a sound that caused his heart to leap into his mouth.

"O-Nami, I have returned."

"Oh, is it you at last?" welcomed the wife.

"How cold it is! Confound those killing winds that blow down from Mt. Asama! O-Nami!"

"Yes; what is it?"

"Whose hat is that?"

"Hat? What hat?"

"Come, no equivocations! There is a strange hat on the floor, and you know whose it is. Out with it! I don't like this underhand way you have acquired of hiding things from me. You are concealing someone in the house!"

"Indeed, no! Why should I want to conceal anyone."

"Then how did this bamboo hat get here? Do you want me to believe that the wind blew it in, as ours is the only building to check its course for miles around? Come, woman, speak up!"

There was a sound of quick movement, and a cry—

"Mercy, mercy . . ."

"Come, speak up or you are a dead woman!"

Kyūsuké, in his hiding in the wood-shed, could imagine the scene.

"This is terrible," he thought. "How could I be such a fool as to forget my hat! It may cost the woman her life!"

The noise in the cottage increased, mingled with the shrieks of the poor woman and the threats of her enraged husband. Kyūsuké stole out of his hiding place and peeped cautiously through a crack in the door. To his horror he found the man was dragging his wife round the room by her long hair with one hand, while he repeatedly struck her with the other. At this sight Kyūsuké forgetting his own fears burst in.

"Sir, sir, all the money I have about me I will give you! The woman is not to blame,—spare her!"

"Who spoke?"

The infuriated man checked his wrath for a moment to stare in astonishment at the unexpected apparition.

Taking advantage of the lull, Kyūsuké quickly produced his hundred *ryō* along with what remained of the money his master had given him for the journey and the little gift.

"Here, good sir, take all—I have no more—and do not punish your wife for a kind action. I only am to blame."

The ruffian took no further notice of his wife whom he left sobbing on the floor, but turned to take up with greedy hands the rich store offered by the traveller. Not content with the money, however, he coolly demanded all the clothes he was wearing and possessed himself of the dagger into the bargain. Poor Kyūsuké! all the earnings of eight hard-working years had gone to fill the pockets of a villainous gentleman of the road.

"In pity, give me back my clothes, I cannot go either back or forward in this naked state," pleaded Kyūsuké. "And my dag-

ger—I need it to defend myself from gentlemen such as you—
though I have nothing of which to be robbed now!" he added
ruefully.

"Take these," said the robber, throwing him a wadded garment and a girdle, both much the worse for wear.

"Thank you very much, but now my dagger . . ."

"That I shall find useful myself."

"But without it I shall be at the mercy of any dog on the
way . . ."

"What a troublesome fellow you are! But no one shall say I
left you without the means of defence. Here, take this, and
begone!"

With these words the robber produced from a cupboard an
old sword doubtless acquired from some former luckless way-
farer and handed it to Kyūsuké, adding:—

"After leaving this house go straight on till you come to a
broad road, follow this always turning to the north and in due
time you will reach Oiwaké. Now go!"

"Again my best thanks," said Kyūsuké bowing low; then turning to the poor woman he said softly:—

"I am very sorry to have brought all this trouble upon you, forgive me."

"No, no, it was I who was to blame but, indeed, I did it for the
best."

"A truce to this nonsense!" cried the robber impatiently.
"Here is a torch to light your way; be off before I change my
mind about letting you go."

"Then, master and mistress, farewell to you," and with these
words Kyūsuké accepted the torch held out to him and hastened
away. But the fates seemed to be still against him, for no sooner
had he set forth than the rain which had begun to come down
in torrents put out his light so that he was in complete darkness.
But this misfortune in reality saved his life, for the robber had
given Kyūsuké a light for no other purpose than that it would
serve his own evil intent, which was to shoot the traveller as
soon as his back was turned. True, he might have despatched
him before he left the cottage, but in that case his wife would

have interfered and been troublesome; besides he hardly liked to turn upon Kyūsuké and murder him just when he had so ungrudgingly given up all he had. Wicked man though he was he could not bring himself to such a dastardly action as that. However, as soon as Kyūsuké closed the door the robber, weapon in hand, softly opened it again and crept out, intending to take aim by the light that Kyūsuké carried. But, alas for him, and fortunately for his intended victim, the heavy rain had extinguished the light; so muttering "lucky dog!" he re-entered his home leaving Kyūsuké to continue his way unmolested.

On arriving at Oiwaké Kyūsuké drew a long breath and congratulated himself on his narrow escape, though how narrow he did not realise. There he gave up his cherished idea of visiting his old home, and determined to retrace his steps to his master's house, begging his way as he had now no money to pay for even the poorest fare. Gonzaemon received him very kindly, though, having heard the details of Kyūsuké's adventure, he could not resist saying:—

"Did I not warn you? If you had drawn a draft for the money as I advised you this would never have happened. But it is too late to talk of that now. You were lucky to escape with the loss of your property,—you might have lost your life as well. Do not give way to despair. Rest for a few days and then set to work again."

While speaking to Kyūsuké the master happened to take up the old sword he had got from the robber. The thread round the hilt was frayed and coming off. He tried to draw the blade but it was so rusty with disuse that it stuck fast in the sheath. Bending over it his eye was caught by the decorative stud which he was convinced was not of brass. Thinking the weapon might be of more value than appeared at first sight, he sent for a dealer in old wares, Kichibei by name, and requested his opinion as to its merits, pretending that it belonged to one of his friends who wished to dispose of it to the best advantage.

The dealer, with the skill acquired by long practice, soon withdrew the blade from its sheath, and after closely examining it for some time, said:—

"The sword is a valuable one. The blade is so rusty that I cannot say anything for certain about it, but the ornamentation is undoubtedly of solid gold. The pommel and stud are of Gotō's engraving, and the guard itself being by Nobuié is worth at least thirty-five *ryō.* I am willing to give one hundred and thirty *ryō* for the decorative parts alone."

These words quite surpassed the expectations of Gonzaemon. He sent the dealer away on the pretext that he would consult his friend, and then told Kyūsuké what he had said.

At this undreamt-of good luck Kyūsuké was struck dumb as well he might be. Gonzaemon, however, encouraged by Kichibei's opinion thought that a Yedo expert might value the sword even more highly and be more able, as well as willing, to purchase it at a higher rate. A blade in so elaborate and rich a mounting could hardly fail to prove a good one; and knowing something of the estimation in which such workmanship was held, he decided to go up to Yedo himself and do the best he could for his faithful but simple servant.

In Yedo he submitted the weapon to the examination of Honami, the ablest connoisseur in matters of this sort, who pronounced the blade to be the undoubted work of Bizen Nagamitsu, one of the ten clever disciples of Masamuné, although the name of the maker was not on it. Further, in proof of his belief he offered to buy it for eight hundred *ryō,* an offer Gonzaemon was more than glad to accept.

The business that took him to the city so satisfactorily concluded, he hastened home with all speed and gave the astonished Kyūsuké an account of the transaction. Laying the money before him he concluded with these words:—

"My dear Kyūsuké, see how advantageous it is to be honest always! Your misfortune has proved a blessing in disguise. Heaven approving of your upright conduct has been pleased to grant you this great favour. How grateful we should be! Now go home again with all despatch, but this time take my advice and do not carry such a large sum in cash."

As soon as Kyūsuké recovered from his surprise he bowed respectfully to his master, and spoke as follows:—

"My good master, you overwhelm me with obligation! I have no words in which to express my feelings. But far be it from me to appropriate all this large sum. I hesitate to displease you, but only one hundred *ryō* do I consider is mine,—for I left the robber's house poorer by just that amount, and that sum I shall send home by money order as you advise. As for the rest, after you deduct the expenses of your journey to Yedo, I shall carry it all to the robber. The sword was his and I can not make myself rich at the expense of a poor highwayman,—that would never do!"

Gonzaemon was struck with admiration at this disinterested conduct on the part of his servant.

"My good fellow," he said warmly, "your honesty puts me to shame! But surely you will not unnecessarily risk your life for such a purpose. As for my journey to Yedo, that is purely my affair and you will dismiss it from your mind. But consider before you act so rashly as to put yourself again into the power of a desperate man."

But Kyūsuké was obstinate as well as honest.

"Far be it from me to go in opposition to your wishes," he said, respectfully, "but in this thing only I beg you to let me have my own way. I am loath to cause you any uneasiness, but villain though he is he will surely not harm a man who comes to do him a good turn. There can be no danger."

Gonzaemon, knowing from experience that further persuasions would be of no avail, reluctantly permitted his servant to do as he proposed. After sending one hundred *ryō* to his father by money order, he tied up the seven hundred *ryō* remaining in a little package, which he put in his bosom and once more set off on his travels. Contrary to his former experience, he had this time no little difficulty in finding the cottage of the highwayman; at last, however, he came to the door which in response to his call was again opened by the kind-hearted mistress. Kyūsuké bowed, and in polite terms thanked her for the favours he received at her hands on a former occasion. The woman was much surprised, but controlling her emotion she said:—

"My good traveller, I do not know how to apologise for what I did to you the other day. Nevertheless you have come again! I shall be still more grieved if you are robbed a second time. Fortunately for you,—though *I* am sorry—my husband is sick in bed. Please make all haste to retrace your steps."

Kyūsuké's kind heart was moved with compassion for the sick man and his wife.

"Indeed I sympathise with you both. Allow me to pay my respects to him and inquire after his health."

"No, no, sir! He is suffering now but his avarice may be excited at the sight of you. Should he again demand all you have with you, you may again be inconvenienced."

"Be quite easy on that score; I am here to bring him some money."

"What do you mean?"

"You are naturally surprised. Let me in and you will know. I must see your husband."

Reluctantly the woman let him come into the house. Making his way to an inner room where the sick man was lying groaning, Kyūsuké, saluting him in the usual manner, inquired:—

"My friend, how are you?"

"This is the traveller you treated so unkindly a short time ago," explained the woman, seeing that her husband did not recognize the visitor.

"Which one?" asked the robber, sourly.

"Sir, it is I. I do not know how to requite you for the kindness you showed me the other day. But now I must tell you what brings me here again."

Thereupon Kyūsuké proceeded to inform the robber of what had happened about the sword, and laying the packet of money by the bed concluded as follows:—

"From the price paid for the sword I have deducted one hundred *ryō* as my due, sending it to my home by money order. All the rest I have brought with me and it is in that package except a small sum I have taken the liberty to keep for my travelling expenses. I have not quite enough to take me to my home in Noto province, and then back to my master's house in Tamamura, Kōdzuké province, so I shall be much obliged if you will kindly allow me a little more. As for the remainder you are welcome to appropriate it all. Ah, how glad I am to be relieved of the charge of this money which has been a source of constant anxiety ever since I set out on this journey."

The sick man appeared to be much impressed by the simple recital of Kyūsuké's tale. After a pause he said:—

"You say your home is in Noto; from what part of the province do you come?"

"I was born in Ogita-mura near Nanao. My name is Kyūsuké and I am the son of a peasant called Kyūzaemon."

"Was your elder brother called Kyūtarō?"

"How do you know that?"

"You may well wonder. Kyūsuké, I have hardly the face to tell you . . . I am Kyūtarō, fallen as you see to the depths of degradation and misery."

"My elder brother, Kyūtarō!"

"With shame I say it, yes."

The two brothers embraced with tears. O-Nami was surprised beyond measure at the pathetic sight.

"Are you indeed my husband's brother? Forgive me, I did not guess it," and she burst into tears.

Kyūsuké hastened to console her.

"I beg you will not cry; forgive my rudeness in not knowing who you were, and forgive also the great trouble I have occasioned you."

Kyūtarō, whose conscience was at last smitten at the thought of all his misdeeds, now took a hunting knife lying within reach, and planted it in the side of his abdomen. His wife and brother, too late to stop the rash act, caught his hands.

"Stop, what madness is this!" cried Kyūsuké.

"My husband, oh what have you done!" exclaimed the wife.

Kyūtarō was almost beyond speaking. In a faint voice he said painfully:—

"Brother, wife, how can I continue to live? Kyūsuké, when I recall how vile I have been I am stricken with remorse and shame. When you were here last I would have killed you, little dreaming you were my brother; O-Nami's remonstrances were of no avail, only providence saved you by miraculously putting out the torch you carried. My evil designs have all turned to your good fortune; the sword I gave you to encourage you the sooner to leave this house proves a precious gift and brings you a large sum of money. Instead of profitting by it you take the trouble to come and give it to me. Kyūsuké, how scrupulous you are! Your nature is honest and spotless as the snow. . . . mine black as charcoal! I have filled up the measure of my wickedness; the disease from which I am now suffering is the punishment of Heaven. What you have just told me will serve like the blessing of a holy priest to enlighten my path to the other world. I am determined to die and join my dead mother,—to offer her my humble apologies for my bad conduct. There is only one thing that disturbs me at this last moment,—it is the thought of O-Nami. It was her misfortune that she married such a wretched husband as I have been, but her heart is pure and tender. Look after her when I am gone—be kind to her, Kyūsuké, I entreat you."

Thus Kyūtarō, unable to bear the stings of an awakened conscience, succeeded in disengaging himself from the arms of his wife and brother and died a manly death.

Kyūsuké and O-Nami mingled their tears over the lifeless body, but the departed spirit was not to be recalled by their lamentations. So they strove to conquer their grief and buried the dead robber in the best manner possible under the circumstances.

Kyūsuké then started for home, taking the money he had brought so far and the hair of the deceased. O-Nami accompanied him. Before leaving the cottage they set fire to it that no one might ever use it for evil purposes again.

On reaching home Kyūsuké told his old father, his stepmother and her daughter, all that had befallen him since he left them so many years before. The hundred *ryō* sent in advance had already come to hand, and he now added to it all the money he had on his person. He also produced the hair of the dead man. Old Kyūzaemon lamented over the sad fate of his undutiful son, but at the same time rejoiced in the possession of so admirable a younger son as Kyūsuké. The step-mother, now repenting of her selfishness of former days, sought his forgiveness. One and all took pity on O-Nami in her great misery. It is wonderful how one man's goodness works upon the hearts of those about him. It was the desire of his relations that Kyūsuké should succeed to his father and carry on the family name; but he firmly declined, and arranged that his step-sister should get a husband, and that the new couple should be the heirs of the old man after his demise. As for O-Nami, she was determined to become a nun and devote her remaining days to religious services for the soul of her dead husband, her sole concern being prayer for the blotting out of his sins. It was decided to build a hermitage for her in order that she might pass her life undisturbed. This is the origin of the Nanao nunnery.

Having settled his family affairs to the satisfaction of all concerned, Kyūsuké was happy to accept out of the cash he had brought home a small sum sufficient to carry him back to his master's home in Kōdzuké province. After recounting his adventures and all he had done, Kyūsuké begged Gonzaemon to reengage him on the same terms as before. Gonzaemon was both surprised and pleased. The praiseworthy actions of Kyūsuké so moved the good-natured village head-man that he proposed to set the young man up as one of his branch families. Kyūsuké's modesty was by no means eager to accept such an honour, but seeing it was really the wish of his patron he at length yielded. I need not tell you how industriously he attended to all his duties that he might prove no discredit to his master's judgment. His family thrives in Tamamura to this day. As for the sword which he got from his robber brother it was purchased by Lord Matsudaira, Daimio of Awa province. He named it "Suté-maru" (a foundling blade) in reference to its history, and treasured it highly. It is still a valued heirloom in the family.